Break Right

Other Books by Erica D. Hearns

Altered before the Altar: Allowing God to Make You
"Meet" to be Met
Altered before the Altar Devotional Study Guide
The Season for Getting Serious: Growing Intimacy with
Christ in Any Season
Jump Start the Journey: Put Pen to Paper, Perfect the
Publishing Process, and Promotion for Propulsion

Break Right

Finding Wholeness in Heartbreak,
and a Good God in a Bad Breakup

Erica D. Hearns

Serious Season Press

BREAK RIGHT: FINDING WHOLENESS IN HEARTBREAK,
AND A GOOD GOD IN A BAD BREAKUP
Serious Season Press

Copyright©2018 by Erica D. Hearns

ISBN: 978-0-9907430-5-7

Cover Design: Norbert Elnar, Masterpiece Movement

Visit www.aseriousseason.com for information regarding discounts, bulk purchases, new releases, and events from Serious Season Press. Email inquiries@aseriousseason.com for additional information.

DEDICATION

To my personal "breakthrough crew[1]," especially Tasha (formerly Jordan) Blomenkamp, the best roomie a girl could ask for when going through major life transitions; Jenny (formerly Calixte) Bullard, one of the most gracious and grounded women I know; and Mom, Pearline Elaine Broyles, who has always been staunchly Team Erica since Day Zero, and who blessed me with the cheekbones and will of a warrior queen.

AND

For every woman going through a difficult season of breaking up, may you live in the light of this truth:

[14] And Jesus returned in the power of the Spirit into Galilee: and there went out a fame of him through all the region round about. [15] And he taught in their synagogues, being glorified of all. [16] And he came to Nazareth, where he had been brought up: and, as his custom was, he went into the synagogue on the sabbath day, and stood up for to read. [17] And there was delivered unto him the book of the prophet Esaias. And when he had opened the book, he found the place where it was written, [18] The Spirit of the Lord is upon me, because he hath anointed me to preach the gospel to the poor; **he hath sent me to heal the brokenhearted,** to preach deliverance to the captives, and recovering of sight to the blind, to set at liberty them that are bruised, [19] To preach the acceptable year of the Lord. [20] And he closed the book, and he gave it again to the minister, and sat down. And the eyes of all them that were in the synagogue were fastened on him. [21] And he began to say unto them, This day is this scripture fulfilled in your ears. ~Lk. 4:14-21 (KJV)

The Lord is near to the brokenhearted and saves the crushed in spirit. Ps. 34:18

---

[1] For a listing of the full breakthrough crew, check out the acknowledgements.

A Breaking Prayer

HEAVENLY FATHER, Creator of Earth and all who dwell herein, Wonderful, Counselor, Redeemer, Provider, longsuffering Savior, and Giver of love who is Love. I acknowledge You and what You can do. I come before You today humbling asking You to break the bondage I find myself bound up in. I know Your word is truth and the truth will set me free. I know who the Son sets free is free indeed. I know I was bought with a price and I shouldn't have made myself the slave or servant of men, but somehow, I forgot. Be merciful to me. Help me to walk in the freedom you've given me.

Break up the bonds yoking me to a dead donkey of a relationship.

Break the bondage of feeling broken. I know You won't refuse a broken and contrite spirit. You will create a clean heart in me and renew a right spirit within me.

Break any hold heartbreak has on Your daughter. Break my heart for what breaks Yours, not for the loss of things You never meant for me to have.

Break any barrier between Your brokenhearted daughter and You. I know You work all things together for my good and Your thoughts toward me are good. You have never left me alone. Only my sins have separated me from You when I refused to repent of them and turn back to You.

Break any bondage of bitterness or betrayal. Help me to acknowledge no one has done anything to me that I haven't done to You when I've sinned against You. Allow me to forgive any wrong done against me, knowing the same measure with which I forgive others You will forgive me.

Break any bondage of blame. Blaming myself or my ex holds me hostage and keeps me from running the race set before me and reaching and pressing toward the mark of the high calling of God through Jesus Christ. Give me a heart that forgives wrong and can pray You don't count the offense to their charge on the last day.

Break the bondage of better than. Keep me from comparing myself to anyone else my ex may choose to date or marry. Keep my heart in perfect peace. Keep my eyes fixed and focused on Jesus. Let me test my own work and not compare it with another, so I can rejoice in myself and not in how much better I believe I am than someone else.

Set ablaze the banners of blameless, beleaguered, broken and beyond repair hanging over my head. I don't have to wear those labels. I take my share of the blame and I lay my broken pieces at Your feet. You bind up the brokenhearted; You don't blame or berate us for breaking our hearts. You are faithful to create new hearts in us.

You have the power to break every bit of bondage binding up the hearts of your daughters. Others will see what You have done for me and glorify You, Father. They will see heartbreak doesn't breakdown the woman who sets her heart and affections on You and commits herself to Your way. Give me the strength to show the world Your people don't break up the way they do. Keep me from seeking to share my side, place blame, or round up sympathizers. Show me how to share Christ and the power of His sacrifice while going through hard times. Allow the world to see Your Son in me even in this, Father.

In the name of Your Son and my savior, Jesus Christ, I pray,

Amen

Contents

PART IV: BREAKAWAY (RUN)

Author's Note

DO YOU REMEMBER the story of the woman with the issue of blood recounted in the gospels? The story is told of a woman who suffered from "an issue of blood"—commonly understood to be menstruation—for twelve years. She spent all the money she had and "suffered many things of many physicians (Mark 5:26 KJV)" to no avail. They could not cure her disease. If this indeed was an issue with her menstrual cycle, according to Mosaic Law, this woman would be separated from society because of her condition. Anything she touched or sat on was unclean. Even if she was cured, she would be isolated for seven more days before she could rejoin society (cf. Lev. 15:19-28). This woman touched Jesus' garment and was made whole.

When Jesus asked, "who touched me?", the woman had a decision to make. She could come forward and share what merely touching Jesus' garment had done for her, or she could remain silent. She had already been made whole and outing herself as a transgressor of the Law of Moses would have serious repercussions. Would she be brave enough to tell the truth of what she'd done?

In the face of great personal cost to herself, the woman came forward. Trembling and afraid, she shared what touching Jesus' garment had done for her. Many came to know the power of Christ and believed on him through the sharing of her experience. After her testimony, Jesus declares her faith has made her whole, and tells her to go and be whole, or healed, of her plague (Mk. 5:34).

Like the woman with the issue of blood before me, there are things I don't want to admit in front of the crowd, but I have to if others are going to see the power of Christ. They are things I must confess for other women to believe in Christ's ability to heal:

- I was in an almost nine-year relationship with my ex with no engagement ring or wedding bells. It makes me sick to my stomach to admit that to you. That fact alone should label me unfit to congregate with single Christian women, let alone talk to them about their romantic lives.

- I should have broken up with my ex years before I did, when some part of me acknowledged and accepted our relationship would never go where I wanted it to go. I should have, but I didn't. I was weak. Who am I to tell you to be strong?

- My ex suggested we "take a break" a year and a half before we broke up. I often think about the consequences of not ending things then. I fight feelings of regret and thoughts of wasted time. I war with "what if" over all the years I sacrificed because I was too afraid to put a limping relationship out of its misery. How can I tell you not to fear the future, to let go of the past and do the hard thing?

I can tell you these things because I'm healed from them. Christ restored me. There may be women who read the above and judge me for brushing up against them in my contaminated state, for daring to touch anything on Jesus with my filthy fingers. But there may also be some "unclean" women who will be emboldened to touch Jesus' garment and be made whole. I have enough faith in Jesus' power to heal that I'm willing to risk the ridicule. I'm willing to write these words with trembling hands and share my story so other women will know they can go to Jesus and be healed, too.

I'm hoping after pouring everything out in this book, Jesus will confirm my wholeness and send me away in peace fully healed. This same hope is what I wish for every woman courageous enough to do the same.

I didn't write this book to bash my ex, belittle our relationship, or portray myself as a martyr. I didn't need over a year and two hundred plus pages to craft a comeback from my breakup. This book is not my Beyoncé moment. It's about as close to **Lemonade** as tap water. I made great use of the safe spaces of prayer, journaling and girl's nights to plop down the things I was tired of carrying a long time ago.

I wrote this book because the thought other women needed to know what God shared with me in the season after my breakup, the notion that maybe God shared those things with me so I could share them with others, wouldn't leave me alone. From the moment I mentioned the possibility of writing this book to a few trusted friends, the response was overwhelming.

Women were willing to rally around this mission of providing single Christian women with a resource for dealing with breakups in a way which would shine their light and inspire those who saw it to glorify God. Many wished they'd had such a resource when they were going through a breakup. Many sisters still recovering from a breakup were eager to dig into such a message.

Breakups are difficult. Experiencing one can be disheartening, especially if you don't have a godly support system. Newly single people don't always consider exhibiting the love of Christ in their hurt state. They don't always experience the peace of God after a breakup. God doesn't always get the glory from the situation.

Sometimes this life interruption, instead of drawing them closer to Christ, pushes them further away. I hope the message of this book moves you closer to God. I know if you draw closer to Him, He will draw close to you.

Throughout this book, I'm going to share as honestly as I can while keeping secret the private details of those who agreed to be a part of my life's story for a season but did not agree to be in this book. What I do disclose is shared to illustrate principles I learned and to encourage you to be as real with yourself as I am being with you. I'm going to challenge you to be honest about your relationship and its demise. At times it may feel as if I'm breaking you down, but I promise you will be built back up better than before.

Introduction

IF YOU'RE READING THIS BOOK, I imagine you're concerned about a woman you love who's struggling with the end of a relationship. Ice cream and Beyoncé songs don't seem strong enough to staunch the tears or battle the blues. The fellowship of the saints may or may not get the brokenhearted out of her uniform of yoga pants or PJs long enough to go do something meaningful that might make her feel better. You can't seem to convince this woman it's worth it to get herself together, even if you stare her in the face every morning as you prepare to wade through another day.

Let me share with you a hard truth that's surprising to no one: breakups suck. Breakups shake up things you thought were settled. This interruption, this loss, can keep you rehearsing your relationship over and over, trying to figure out exactly where it went wrong. Even though the facts are simple, getting a firm grasp on them is like trying to hold on to a greased-up pig. Family and friends grow tired of hearing the same song on repeat and tune out or change the channel every time they hear the opening chords of this conversation.

Breakups force you out of your comfort zone. The person you thought would always be there suddenly isn't. The things you depended on him to do are suddenly your responsibility. You may have to find new ways to de-stress after a long day or someone else to go to the movies or dinner with on the weekends.

At some point you may find yourself back in "the dating pool." You may discover this "pool" is so shallow your feet aren't covered. The foolishness you encounter and the seemingly endless parade of horrible first dates may make you rethink ending things with your ex. At the very least, you may find yourself questioning why you bothered to shave your legs, dress up, and/or leave your house.

If you've been obedient to the gospel, you've been made new in Christ. You should be renewing your mind constantly. You should be maintaining your body, so it doesn't break down until it's time to rest in God with the knowledge He will exchange it for an incorruptible one.

With all this newness and life, friend, are you breaking down? If you are, why is that? Is it because you aren't being built up anymore? Are you hiding the old, worn out and ugly instead of letting God redeem and renew you? Are you settling for the corruptible junk in your life instead of exchanging it for the incorruptible God has for you?

In breakups, it can be difficult, almost impossible, to gain perspective. It's easy to become so wrapped up in rewriting history, making your ex the villain and yourself the saint, that you miss the truth the relationship revealed to you. Your breakup isn't a story for you to drastically alter to garner sympathy, incite righteous anger, or be praised for your ability to hang in until the end or hang it up.

The purpose of a breakup is to interrupt a pattern, to reveal a fallacy and invite you to find the truth. The things you've experienced in the past, including a breakup, can still hurt today and in the future. You can try to outrun your pain, or you can choose to learn the lesson and avoid repeating the mistake in the future (a wise mandrill baboon in a Disney movie taught me that).

A person can experience many different "breaks" in life, and in the second half of 2016, I experienced several. I lost my job, broke up with my boyfriend, and my lease was shortened. I was newly single, jobless, and about to be homeless in a short amount of time.

It was during this dark period where I went from one bad breakup to another that God began revealing to me the truths I detail in this book. He began to shift my perspective and change my heart in ways that have revolutionized how I approach the hardships in my life.

This excerpt from a blog post I wrote in 2016 best illustrates this shift:

> ...A successful outcome isn't always the desired outcome...
>
> Many of the things I would have seen as major failures or disappointments before were actually invitations and opportunities to stop, reflect, and take stock of where I was and where I wanted to go. In this season of tremendous growth, I looked for opportunities to uncover a truer sense of self hidden in the dirt of what the world classifies as failure. Once I understood the true meaning of success, major fails became major opportunities...
>
> - ~~I broke up with my boyfriend.~~ I received the long-awaited answer to a long and painful prayer, a la Sarah McLachlan. After almost nine years of dating, my relationship ended with an awkward conversation in the church parking lot the day after the Presidential election. An end of an era. A historically poignant moment to hang a memory on...
>
> I prayed for this! Again, this wasn't the desired result, but **God answered a prayer I've prayed for years this year.** As painful as the answer may be, it wasn't a sucker punch in a parking lot, but gentle nudges and a calm voice saying, "it's time."

God has been incredibly gentle with my heart during this time. What once would've started an epic search to figure out what was wrong with me...gave me peace. It also gave me an invitation. My soul asked me on a date. Who was Erica, 31, single, Christian, no kids? What parts of myself have been pushed down, lost, or ignored in the last nearly nine years?

It's been fun rediscovering who I am, spending more time with myself and my family, friends, and God. I said yes to things I wouldn't have before, and no to things I wouldn't have before.

It hasn't all been roses. One doesn't spend so many years getting to know someone, investing in a shared future, and end it with no hurts or regrets. **One doesn't sit with oneself and examine one's heart this closely without seeing some ugly things embedded there.** When two great catches don't catch each other, it's bewildering and sad... **How amazing it was to see the preparation He put me through to be able to walk this season out in front of so many to His glory!**

This book was born from a radical notion: how can I be more like Christ and shine my light before men while going through something as taxing and hurtful as a breakup?

Once I began pursuing this idea, people noticed a change in me. What was happening on the inside of me began changing me on the outside as well. My skin was clear. I had a glow of peace about me. People asked "Didn't you just end a long-term relationship? How are you handling this so calmly and peacefully?"

When people asked these questions, I was able to tell them they were witnessing the fruit of focusing on my relationship with God. I was able to share the perspective God had given me. Having these openings to proclaim Christ to people and/or confirm what they already believed about the Lord proved that even in a breakup, there are opportunities to show the Lord.

This book aims to shift your perspective of the breakups you've suffered in your life. I pray it allows me to do what many of your friends and family can't or won't do: hold your hand and handle your heart with humble care; hand you tissues and hug your neck; all while I call you out on your conceit and cancel your pity party (trust me, you were the only one excited about attending). My desire is to help you find wholeness in the middle of your heartbreak, not on the other side, and to point out the good God who's with you in the middle of this bad breakup.

A broken heart is deeper than people give it credit for. It can change the trajectory of a life. It's no small matter to God when your heart is broken. Whether you feel your heartbreak is minor or major, God sees what you're going through. He longs to be close to you and bind up your wounds.

This book, while meant to be a balm and a comfort, a written account of God's lovingkindness toward me and others in a difficult season, was also written to encourage women to be a light in their own dark night. I hope hearing about how I walked through my recent breakup helps you feel less alone in what you're going through. I want you to heal, and if this book helps you do that, I'll feel blessed to have been a part of your healing. But my biggest hope is for this trial, tribulation, or unfortunate uncoupling to matter and mean something far beyond you and me.

I don't want any part of my journey or yours to be a wasted experience. I want to say I used every opportunity my breakup presented to show Christ, experience His transformative power for myself and encourage others to do the same. I want to experience how God's strength is made perfect in my weakness, and for other women to have the same encounter with the Lord.

A breakup is a unique opportunity to witness God work through heartache and suffering. Working through trials and tribulations will mature you and ensure you lack nothing. In other words, you will be complete, entire, **whole.** I want that wholeness for you.

You should know wholeness is not on the other side of coming to terms with your breakup, nor is it found on the last page of this book. Wholeness is the product of a tested faith, the perfect work of patience. I can't predict when you will feel whole; for me, it wasn't after I fully healed from heartbreak, but in the middle of it. I became aware of my wholeness when I realized my faith was still intact after being stripped of several false identities, including that of being my ex's girlfriend.

I didn't achieve wholeness; I discovered my wholeness. I realized I wasn't lacking any good thing. God hadn't held back good gifts from me.

I don't have a 10-point program or "path to wholeness" for you to follow. The truth is you don't have to chase after wholeness in this season. Let your faith be tried so it produces patience, and let that patience grow to maturity so you can experience wholeness.

Right now, what matters most is what God is doing in you. What matters most is having the opportunity to reflect the light of His truth into this dark world. What matters most is someone seeing the difference God makes in your messy situation. Anyone can be fine and speak well of their ex after they find someone new or enter a relationship, but being at peace and shining in the midst of the darkest part of this experience is rare. It will grab attention. People will want to know how you're shining, and you'll have the opportunity to share Christ.

Let's be honest: you put your heart into a relationship and it didn't work. You don't have a ring or a husband to show for all you invested. That's painful, and quite possibly embarrassing.

But maybe, if you shift the focus off what you didn't get and onto who God is whether you get what you want or not, someone will see God and glorify Him. Maybe by focusing on Christ, your feet can find the path God wants you to walk, the purpose He designed specifically for you. Now that you're not tied to or yoked up with someone He never wanted you bound to, you're free to go where He sends and do what He says.

When I *broke up*
with my ex,
I didn't realize
anything other than the
relationship was
broken

These are the Breaks

It's *funny* how "*break*" can mean "*rest*," but a *rested* person isn't "*broken*"

"BREAK" IS A FUNNY WORD. Its definition depends on its context. Breaks can be things or actions. They can be made, taken, or experienced. You can rest in one, run for one, or be ripped apart by one. A break can be good, feel bad, and look ugly all at the same time.

No matter what kind of break it is, a break is always jarring. It's a disruption of the status quo, a departure from the norm, a deviation that never seems standard. Knowing a break is coming doesn't make it any less jarring.

This is especially true when a romantic breakup occurs. The types of breaks one experiences when a relationship ends vary based on the individual, the relationship, and even day to day. The purpose of this section is to provide context to define the possible breaks a breakup could entail and techniques for dealing with the immediate fallout from the initial breakup.

Unfortunately, my breakup wasn't the first time I suffered through a painful break. When it comes to painful breaks, I am in a class by myself. Physically, I've broken bones, suffered sprains, jammed fingers and otherwise proven when it comes to protecting my appendages, I am wholly inadequate.

While physical and romantic breaks aren't the only ones to befall me, they best illustrate the reasons things have broken in my life and the lessons to be taken from those moments. Most of my breaks have come from reaching for something and missing, trying something new, or getting distracted. They've been exacerbated by struggles with indecision or attempts to avoid the inevitable.

Maybe many of the breaks you've experienced have resulted from similar causes. Hopefully the stories I relate of some of my most painful injuries, physical and romantic, and the lessons I've learned, will be instructive and shift your perspective.

Take Heed Lest You Fall

WHEN I WAS IN MIDDLE SCHOOL, I fell off my bike and broke my wrist. It happened while I was riding by a popular teen hangout, the Holland Center. The Wallace E. Holland Center was a civic center where guys played basketball outside in the summer.

I had a clear purpose when I set out toward the Holland Center that day in my cut off jean shorts and lycra top: catch my crush's eye. If I snagged the interest of another cute boy or two, that was fine by me. I was tired of seeing and not being seen. Today, my crush was going to notice me.

Manicured lawns flashed by on my right without making an impression on me. My eyes were focused on the center coming up on my left. I craned my neck to see who was on the court and if they would turn to see me ride by. Every now and then, my eyes swept forward to make sure I didn't run over anyone, but for the most part, my attention was on what was happening across from me.

At the corner parallel to the basketball court sat a house whose front yard sloped down to the sidewalk. A little trench, less than an inch wide, ran between the sidewalk and the lawn. I imagine its purpose was to catch water runoff. That day as I rode past, my bike swerved to the left and it caught something else—my front tire.

One of the few principles of physics I know well is that an object in motion tends to stay in motion. When my front tire stopped, my body kept going. To my recollection, I was bucked off the back of my bike like a bull rider. One minute I was riding my bike, and the next I was on my back on the sidewalk looking at the sky.

In that moment, I didn't feel pain; I felt embarrassment. Who saw that? I wondered. I had fallen off my bike like a little kid across the street from a bunch of bare chested, basketball playing boys—boys I went to school with or who lived in my neighborhood. If any of them saw me fall, I couldn't show my face anywhere ever again.

I didn't realize anything other than my ego was injured until I tried to stand. When I put my right hand down and attempted to push myself up, pain shot up my arm like fire. I stood as quickly as I could, freed my bike tire, and jumped back on. I tried to steer with both hands, but it quickly became apparent I was more severely injured than I thought.

As I rode home one handed, my wrist swelled so much the skin popped open. Dark bruises shaped like fingers began to form across my inner wrist. I didn't know what the damage was, but I knew I had to get help.

Looking back, my break up and breaking my wrist both had similar root causes and evoked similar reactions in me. When my relationship ended, I wasn't focused on where it was going anymore. I had taken my eyes off where I was heading. Instead, I was looking at other people, wondering if they could see what was really going on with me and my relationship. I was focused on silencing critics of my relationship and how long it was taking us to get engaged. Occasionally I checked in front of me to see where this might be going, but what was happening outside of my relationship was much more interesting than the fruitless ring watch holding pattern we were in.

When I had the talk with my ex that ended our relationship, the talk didn't take me by surprise as much as the result did. Just like I knew the house on the corner had that little ditch dug along the sidewalk, I knew our relationship had reached a fork in the proverbial road. I knew what my ex wanted to talk about and why, but the reality was jarring.

Also similar to breaking my wrist, when I broke up with my ex, I didn't realize anything other than the relationship was broken. I had peace about the relationship ending. It wasn't what I wanted, but I had accepted it before it happened. Yet, months later I discovered things that hurt when I tried to use them.

I don't know the circumstances behind your breakup. I don't know who broke up with whom or why the relationship ended. I can't say if you never saw it coming because you weren't paying attention or knew things had to end. Your relationship could have ended amicably or acrimoniously. I'm none the wiser about any of the facts.

But the feelings? The range of emotions that other people don't seem to get? I'm intimately acquainted with those. The battle between the rational and emotional sides of your brain? I'm on a first name basis with both parties. The slow creep of pain and the sudden sharpness of it when you discover a new area of sensitivity? We're so close, we have our own inside jokes.

Maybe like me when I fell off my bike, you were more concerned with who saw you fall than what you might have broken. Perhaps you're only beginning to realize the extent of your injuries. If so, this section will be an eye opener. It will shed light on the situation to help you assess what's been broken or damaged in your breakup.

A break can *be good,*

feel bad,

and

look ugly

all at the

same time.

The Struggle is Real

What did you struggle with after the break up?

I struggled a lot with trying to analyze everything and figure out how and why we ended up where we ended up, especially because we had at one point been talking about marriage and a future, and the initial unraveling of our relationship kind of happened out of the blue.

I also struggled with some big faith questions, because I had been waiting and praying for a godly relationship for many years, and he truly seemed like the answer to that prayer. When things unraveled, it was hard for me to see where God was in all of that, and it was hard for me to return to singleness again.
💔 Katie H.

I struggled with feeling like I would ever be able to trust a man again. I sought therapy and am still working on my confidence so that I don't continue to date men I know in the very beginning are wrong for me. There were so many red flags that I ignored because I thought we had a good connection and I didn't want to be alone.
💔 Kacy S.

After the breakup I struggled with the idea that I would never love someone like that again or that I would ever get over them. I was like 22 and it just felt like I would always have this love in my heart for that person, but I can tell you that 10 years down the road that is not even remotely true.

💔 Natalie M.L.

The main struggle was trying to figure out why we got together in the first place (a different long story) and why things seemed to be going so well in the beginning if it wasn't meant to be. I personally also struggled with him dating and God sending the one for him not too long after our breakup while I remained single with no interests.

💔 Ayanna S.

I struggled with deep brokenness and insecurity after the breakup. This was at a point in my life where I was finding my identity and security in guys, and because I saw myself being with this guy for the rest of my life, this breakup really shook me to the core of who I was. I struggled with my sense of worth and who I was as a person.

💔 Erica U.

Immediately after he asked for the divorce, I found out I was pregnant, so I struggled most with understanding why the Lord would let this happen how it did, how my husband could still walk out on me during the time when I needed him the most, and what the heck my life would look like as a single parent from the day my child was born. I was also very concerned with how I would explain what happened to our friends and family. We had been together for nearly 10 years.

🖤 Kelsey B.

The death of the marriage. His smell in my bedroom, which I couldn't sleep in for months. The looks from the members of my church family.

There were so many ladies who reached out to me and was honestly there for me bearing this burden. There are some who almost avoid me. I am not sure if they just don't know what to say or [would] rather stay out of it. I also know of some who feel as though divorce is wrong under any circumstance and avoid me because I was the one that filed for divorce. That was a struggle for me because I felt as though regardless of who filed, if the fact that he was unfaithful is enough for God for me to walk away, why is it so hard for my church family to understand that?

That is no longer a struggle for me. The church family that has always been there for me is what matters. We often spend too much time focused on those who don't rather than those who do.

🖤 Cheryl S.

The thought of us never being together again.

🖤 Andreana J.

evaluate
whether you should
replace,

repair,

or *rejoice over*

what's been
broken.

The Breaks

WHEN YOU SUFFER AN INJURY, the first priority of those treating you is to determine where the injury is located and its severity. After a breakup, many women have one of two responses: they will become introspective and seek to understand what's happened, or they will push themselves physically or mentally to succeed, leaving no time for reflection. Neither of these approaches addresses the primary needs of the woman as well as you might think.

Introspection and reflection, without wise counsel, the Word of God, and action steps, usually devolves into self-flagellation or self-justification. It can lead to emotional martyrdom, a negative bias toward men, or being trapped in a painful cycle of insecurity and overthinking.

Alternately, pushing down your feelings and stuffing your schedule is equally detrimental. This can lead to mental and physical exhaustion, fatigue, and isolation. When you push yourself so hard to succeed in other spheres of life to prove you can do something right, setbacks and failures become magnified. Instead of your product not selling or your pitch not being chosen, you may feel as if you were passed over or not good enough.

While these approaches may identify the location and severity of your major injury, they don't identify them all, nor do they provide useful information about treatment. If you're going to break right, you need to inventory what's broken. Further, you need to evaluate whether you need to replace, repair, or rejoice over what's been broken.

Right now, it may feel like everything is broken. It's either shattered in a million pieces at your feet or hasn't worked right since you broke up with your ex. Or maybe you feel like nothing is broken. Some of your possessions may be banged up or chipped, but everything still works. Neither of these impressions is accurate.

Brokenness is a good indicator of investment. If a breakup broke everything in you, it indicates you invested more of yourself than you should have. If ending a relationship didn't interrupt anything in your life, you weren't invested enough in the relationship.

These conclusions may seem harsh, but they're accurate. I fought battles on each of these battlegrounds: introspective and outward focused, feeling like everything was intact and like everything I was had been smashed or trashed. I know the fallacy of both approaches and the inaccuracy of both evaluations from experience. Believe me when I tell you they are all vanity and grasping for the wind. They are all "me" centric. They all require me to fix myself or declare myself fine when I can't heal myself. You can't, either.

The truth is, we take stock of where we are and what we have left, and we depend on God to give the increase. God is the one who heals hearts.

You should know at this early stage that this book can't heal you. It won't repair everything that's damaged. It can't replace everything your ex took or the relationship broke. It can't return what you lost a hundredfold. But my hope is to help point you to the

One who can do all those things exceeding abundantly above all that could ask or imagine (Eph. 3:20).

This section will help you identify the ideals, identities and/or interactions that may have broken when your relationship ended. Like x-rays and examinations, the process of discovering what's broken is painful. It shouldn't end with self-evaluation, either. Many of the breaks you find won't be simple ones and will need specialists to repair and set.

There's more than one way to break a relationship...or a heart. There's more that can be broken by ending a relationship than your heart. Just like there are multiple kinds of breaks a bone can suffer, there are multiple types of relationship breaks:

FRACTURES

Fractures aren't complete breaks. They're cracks. These cracks may be small, but they can be painful, especially when several occur in a small area. If you find an area has fractures, you have to decide if you will cover the area and allow it to heal, or if it needs to be broken for real healing to occur.

CLEAN BREAK

A clean break happens when there is a clear separation. When you don't have children, property, or pets together, the relationship can be easily terminated. You don't have to file paperwork or move when the relationship ends. When you break up with your ex, you no longer need to interact with him.

💔 COMPLICATED BREAK (1)

A complicated break occurs when you worship or work with someone. It may be difficult to avoid interacting with your ex in these environments. Other people who worship or work with you may voice opinions and beliefs about the ending of your relationship that make you and/or your ex feel ostracized. Your livelihood and/or spiritual life will be affected by the decisions you make regarding your future interactions with these locations and your ex.

💔 COMPLICATED BREAK (2)

A more complicated break makes separating a more delicate process because you still need to maintain a level of communication with your ex, even if only for a limited amount of time. If you lived with your ex, were married to them, and/or have a child or children with them, you will experience a more complicated break. If you own property together or share a pet, you may also experience a complicated break.

A word of encouragement before you begin excavating your heart: not every broken thing needs to be mourned over. As I said earlier, some are to be rejoiced over. Hopefully many of the bad habits and hang-ups you acquired are shattered. Prayerfully false identities have been smashed. Each toxic or unhealthy bond that's already broken is one less to agonize over getting rid of later. Each broken false identity or ideal is one less perspective shift to make.

Another word of encouragement: not everything on this list will be broken for you. Many of your positive personality traits or beliefs may be intact. You may discover your heart isn't broken, or that most of the broken items are a cause for celebration. Don't delay diving in because you're scared of what might be broken; focus on finding what's still whole.

Carefully examine each area. Don't discount any offhand. Search yourself. Be honest with yourself. Gather information on areas you need to address. Pay special attention when they come up later in the book.

💔 CONNECTION WITH YOUR EX

When you end a relationship, the connection between you and your ex is severed. Your relationship is irrevocably changed. Even if you decide to get back together or to remain friends, your connection with them will never be the same.

💔 TIME

When a relationship ends, you may feel you lost or wasted time. Time is a precious commodity for all of us. No one knows how much time they have. The time we choose to spend engaged in an activity is time we can't spend doing other things. Each expenditure of time is an investment, a choice with a cost or risk attached to it. Like any investment, if the return isn't what we hoped, we can feel cheated.

It's painful to think you wasted a significant amount of your time engaged in an unprofitable relationship. It's easy to obsess over all the things you could have done with your time if you hadn't been "throwing it away." When you do this, you're throwing good time after bad. You can't get a refund on your time. Obsessing over lost time robs you of the time you currently have.

If you learned from the experience, consider the time spent in your last relationship an investment in your education. Time is the currency used to pay for lessons in emotional and spiritual maturity. Make the most of your investment. Learn the lessons. Get the maturity you paid for.

💔 PICKER

A bad relationship can convince you that your "picker" is broken. You can feel as if you lack the ability to discern and choose a suitable mate for yourself. Maybe you thought you knew exactly what you needed and wanted in a relationship. Perhaps you thought you might have found it when you started dating your ex. You thought you knew where the relationship would go, but it didn't go there. This may lead you to question your judgment. Have I chosen the right people to populate my life? Am I a good judge of how someone feels about me or my place in their life? Do I really know why this person was in my life?

💔 IDENTITY (FALSE)

One of the few indisputably positive breaks that can occur when you experience a breakup is the breaking of a false or fake identity. A false identity is usually attached to and constructed around a label which describes what you do or who you love without addressing the core of who you are. When you attempt to give your existence a meaning or definition using these markers, your true identity gets buried beneath the labels.

If you're willing to be honest about what identities you assumed to accommodate your ex, you can come out of your breakup a more authentic version of yourself. The broken identity of being so and so's girlfriend, and the removal of identity labels that aren't integral to who you are can save your life as surely as cutting off a trapped or infected limb can save the rest of the body.

❤ EGO/EXPECTATIONS

Some of the symptoms you may attribute to a broken heart might be caused by a bruised ego or shattered expectations. Your ego will convince you you're the perfect match for someone and they can't do any better. You did everything right and were the perfect girlfriend. You knew you were "the one" for him; you were just waiting for him to catch up and put a ring on your finger.

Regardless of whether he "put a ring on it," making you a fiancée or wife, or your left ring finger felt a distinctive draft, you committed to his team. Maybe you invested time in getting him together. You made him a better dresser, found him a better barber, or pushed him to pursue the degree or certification he needed to reach the next level. You're the type of woman who elevates her man and helps him "level up" in life. You're a good thing. The best thing. Until the relationship ends.

For the record, I don't think there's anything wrong with being confident in what you bring to the table. There's also nothing wrong with investing in the personal growth of the person you are in a relationship with. I'm merely pointing out the possibility that your ego took the brunt of your breakup, not your heart.

If you're angrier about who broke up with whom or what his new girlfriend looks like or has in comparison to you, it may be your ego talking. Your ego throws around statements about what you "deserve," and how you were "the best thing that ever happened to him." Ego reveals if your investment was in the person, or your future with them.

Although not a break, a bruised ego is still a painful injury. However, it might be a necessary one. Humbling ourselves is a good thing. Pride, another expression of ego, goes before a fall (Prov. 16:18). It would behoove us to recognize if ego is churning up feelings of anger, resentment, or bitterness in the wake of a breakup.

Closely associated with ego is expectation. When ego convinces you that you deserve something, you can start to build expectations around its attainment. You fantasize about how and when he might propose. You paint a glamorized picture of your life together—the trips you'll take, the kids you'll have, the house you'll live in. While there's nothing wrong with seeing a future with someone, the wise woman ascribes to what James says:

> Go to now, ye that say, Today or tomorrow we will go into such a city, and continue there a year, and buy and sell, and get gain: Whereas ye know not what shall be on the morrow. For what is your life? It is even a vapor, that appeareth for a little time, and then vanisheth away. For that ye ought to say, If the Lord will, we shall live, and do this, or that. James 4:13-15 KJV

Everyone has hopes and dreams for their future. Christians the world over make plans. But were your plans made in consideration of what the Lord's will for your life might be? Did your plans hinge on Him, the Lord, and what He wants, or did they hinge on him, the guy you were dating?

When you're committed to living an "if the Lord will" life, taking an unexpected turn off the road you thought would lead to marriage hurts. What hurts worse, though, is willfully ignoring God's directions and being routed back by Him. Following your plans and chasing your expectations can lead to time stuck in transit, going nowhere, and random detours. It adds time and mileage to an otherwise short trip.

♥ HEART

"Hearts Get Broken All the Time (But the Problem is, This Time It's Mine)" is more than a song by the late, great Luther Vandross. For many, it's a true representation of how they feel after a breakup. They feel as if their heart is broken, shattered into a million pieces. Their chest hurts. They can't stop crying. Getting through the day requires more stamina than they can muster. Pictures, a string of text messages, old DMs, songs—anything can set off the ticking time bomb in their chest.

I'm not here to downplay your feelings or to tell you to pull it together. If you say your heart is broken, I believe you. Emotional trauma is real. The breaking of a bond involves severing, and severing is painful. I'm not discounting that. At. All.

I imagine Job was heartbroken when he lost his children, livestock, and health. His grief was so great, his friends sat by him for seven days and nights without speaking a word.

I can only hope you have friends in your life who would understand that sometimes words are inadequate, but their presence is appreciated. I'm not going to pretend I have the language to speak to every possible way in which your heart has been broken by the ending of your relationship. Consider this paragraph my moment of sitting in silence and solidarity with you.

I have a confession to make: after my breakup, I didn't feel heartbroken. The fact I didn't feel brokenhearted after ending a nearly nine-year relationship unsettled me. Don't misunderstand me: I felt pain, disillusionment, and hurt. I knew I was broken in several places. But my heart didn't appear to be one of them. While studying and thinking about my feelings, this scripture got stuck in my heart:

> Lay not up for yourselves treasures upon earth, where moth and rust doth corrupt, and where thieves break through and steal: But lay up for yourselves treasure in heaven, where neither moth nor rust doth corrupt, and where thieves do not break through nor steal: For where your treasure is, there will your heart be also. Matt. 6:19-21 KJV

This scripture is very convicting to me. Where was my treasure? If my treasure had been in my relationship, my heart would have been there. If my heart was in that relationship, it would have broken along with the relationship.

I know it may seem crass or unfeeling of me to ask you this right now, but is your heart really broken? Are you sure it's not your ego, expectations, or plans that have been broken? If your heart is broken, is it because you laid up your treasures on earth, in your relationship?

The good news is if your heart was broken, God is near to you. He can create in you a clean heart, shiny and new. If you repent, or turn to Him, and confess, He will restore. If your heart isn't broken, maybe it's because it was in the right place.

♥ BELIEF IN LOVE

Your belief in love can be broken by a bad breakup. You may think true love doesn't exist, or if it does, you'll never find it. You can become cynical and hardened by repeated disappointments in love. People who are disillusioned with love categorize it as a game, a myth, or a lie. They view their disillusionment as enlightenment, a sign of maturity.

If you no longer believe in love, dear heart, your feet are set in slippery places. Love is not the property of those experiencing the bliss of partnership with another human being. God is love (I John 4:8). God's word exhorts believers to love one another because love is of God (I John 4:7). Jesus says people will know His disciples by their love one for another (John 13:35).

A breakup can break and rob you of many things, but don't let it take your belief in love. Everything written about love in 1 Corinthians 13 and 1 John is still true today. 1 Corinthians 13 is not a romantic rubric to spout at a wedding like a poem or reading. Read it in context. Read it with the knowledge God is love, gives love, and calls us to love. I guarantee it will shift your perspective.

💔 TRUST

Many women find themselves struggling to trust when a romantic relationship ends. These women expect men to lie about everything from their relationship status to their intentions. When your trust is broken, you don't believe anything until you see it. Everything must be verified and notarized in triplicate. You watch everything a person says and does, looking for inconsistencies. You're always ready to cut ties if anything doesn't seem above board.

I understand this reaction. You've been hurt. It's natural to seek to avoid experiencing the same pain in the future. But such hypervigilance and a "one and done" mentality is highlighting brokenness.

A lack of trust paired with a swiftness to cut people off is a sign you're unforgiving. Forgiveness involves reconciliation and a willingness to forget the offense. A marked lack of trust underlines the fact forgiveness hasn't occurred. Being unforgiving is a precarious place to be. If we don't forgive others, God will not forgive us (Matt. 6:14-15).

💔 IDENTITY (TRUE)/SPIRIT (MENTAL)

When some women end relationships, they look in the mirror and find they no longer recognize themselves. During their association with their ex, their boundaries, the lines they thought they would never cross, may have shifted. Their sense of knowing the kind of person they are, the things they would and wouldn't do, may be compromised. Their self-respect might be shattered by the realization they didn't hold fast to the things they said were important.

A person whose sense of self is broken has a broken spirit. This broken spirit robs them of their will to fight for their personhood. Their resistance to conformity is shattered.

Your relationship could have broken your spirit. Perhaps you acquiesced and assimilated your self-image into what your ex seemed to want you to be. Now that you're without him, you don't know who you're supposed to be anymore. Who you are at your core is unrecognizable.

This is a difficult break to bounce back from. If you feel this ashamed, this broken, how likely are you to ask God for His forgiveness? How likely are you to believe you've been forgiven?

A good example of a broken identity and spirit is Samson. Samson lost something integral to him, something God proclaimed about him before he was born. His parents prepared for this gift of God by eating and living according to God's instruction while Samson was in the womb. Once he was born, they fed and cared for him the way God instructed.

Samson went against everything he knew about who he was to pursue the Philistine woman and Delilah. He loses his strength as a result.

Samson knew where His strength came from. When he misled Delilah about the source of his strength, she always sought to take it from him. Yet eventually he tells her its true source.

For years, I thought I was better than Samson. I wondered why, after Delilah showed him several times what she was about, he chose to tell her the source of his strength. Then I experienced being in a relationship. I saw signs my ex wasn't the right man for me and stayed. I turned a blind eye. I ignored. I waved off. I kept placing my trust in a relationship I felt too invested in to end. All of a sudden, Samson was deserving of grace in my eyes.

Whatever led Samson to tell Delilah the source of his strength, the consequences were devastating. He lost his strength. His eyes were blinded. He was forced into servitude. His enemies had a feast celebrating his downfall. Imagine how defeated he must have felt.

But instead of staying defeated, Samson cried out to God. Crying out to God is integral in fixing anything we feel is broken, but especially a broken spirit. Who else can tell us who we were meant to be? Who else can confirm our true identity?

💔 SPIRIT (SPIRITUAL)

There is another way to view a broken spirit. Your sense of self may be intact, but your spirit is broken over sins you committed during or after your relationship. The realization you've done something you said you never would do, broken laws you said you would never break, or violated a relationship you never thought you would violate can break your spirit. You feel broken and contrite.

Have you ever broken something delicate and fragile because you mishandled it? Maybe you didn't have a secure grip on it and fumbled it. You lunged and twisted, trying with everything in you to catch it, to save it, but it broke at your feet. That's a hurting feeling. You would give anything to take back your clumsiness. You wonder "why did I do that?" You're sorry. You want to fix it, but it's broken in ways you don't know how to fix.

Our spirits can be broken in this manner when we sin. When we sin, we mishandle the precious gift of salvation God has given us through Jesus' death on the cross. Often, we think there's no hope of restoration after what we've done, no way to fix what we've broken, but God says otherwise.

David states in Psalm 51 that God will not refuse a broken and contrite spirit (v. 17). Take your broken pieces to God. Tell Him, "God, I broke this, and I don't know how to fix it."

If your spirit is broken over sin, then you need to repent. Repentance is more than being sorry. It's a repositioning. It's turning away from sin. Next, confess your sin to the Lord. In 1 John 1:9, the bible says if we confess our sins, God is faithful to forgive our sins and to cleanse us from all unrighteousness.

💔 SENSE OF SECURITY/ SAFETY/STABILITY

A broken relationship can lead to a broken sense of security and safety. This sense of safety and security can be physical, mental, emotional, and/or financial. A breakup can shake up where you live, worship, and/or shop. If you have a child with your ex, the end of the relationship can change how you parent with him and strip your child of their sense of security.

Everyone wants to feel secure and safe. No one wants to feel the burden of not being able to pay bills or feel safe in the neighborhood they live in. We all want to worship where we feel God is being taught and glorified and we feel welcome. Most people want to believe they are worth loving and will find love. But not everyone has these assurances.

I've experienced many moments in which my stability and sense of security have been shaken. I know what it's like to live on faith. I've fought off fear and asked God to help my unbelief when bills came in and money didn't. In the midst of my struggles, I held on to a core belief: I don't know how things are going to work out or what's going to happen, but I know God will take care of me. I had to make adjustments, but I knew God wouldn't leave me alone. I would find employment, have a home and fulfilling relationships, and maybe somewhere along the line a romantic relationship. I wasn't going to be left out in the elements.

If you were living with your ex or dependent on them for all or part of your financial, physical, or emotional security, you will have to adjust. You may have to move, find a job, and figure out how you're going to eat this week, all while dealing with the demise of your relationship. But if I could lose my job with the end of my lease looming and then breakup with my ex, you can, too.

I don't have a special "anointing" or gift from God you can't access. But I understand why you may feel like this sort of faith is far from your reach. This can be an indication that the loss of your sense of security has fractured or broken your relationship with God, or your belief His thoughts toward you are good.

💔 RELATIONSHIP WITH GOD/FAITH IN GOD'S PLAN

Some people lose their relationship with God when they lose their relationship with a significant other. They no longer believe God has good plans for their life. They're no longer convinced it matters if they spend time with Him or if they attend worship services or bible studies. They may still believe in God, but they stop pursuing a relationship with Him.

This loss of relationship doesn't have to be immediate or all at once. It can occur over time. Maybe you decide to switch congregations to avoid your ex but can't seem to find where you fit. Maybe you associate going to service too closely with your ex, so you decide to stay home and worship God by yourself. Over time, you feel your relationship with God eroding. You aren't praying as much as you were. You try to read the bible, but you find your focus drifting. You rush through interactions with God, treating Him more like the cashier at the grocery store than the loving Savior He is.

Our relationship with God can't be tied to a person—not a minister, elder, strong brother or sister in the church, our parents, or our ex. Any of those people can fail us or leave us. People move out of town, fall away from the church, or pass away. People change.

God doesn't change. He doesn't leave us. He doesn't want "by proxy" faith; He wants a close, intimate relationship with each of us.

Your belief in God and assurance He wants good things for your life should be based on His word, not the words of any human being. Your love for Him should be based on His actions, sending Jesus to die on the cross for your sin, not on the actions of your ex or anyone else. Base your belief in who God is and what He wills on His word, not your feelings for, or experiences with, anyone else.

💔 BROKEN BELIEF SYSTEMS

Relationships will test you and show you if you really believe what you say you believe. They will reveal what concepts or buzzwords you've latched on to that you don't understand or wrongfully apply.

IT ISN'T BROKEN, BUT DO YOU NEED TO FIX IT?

Not everything forged in your relationship is broken when you break up. When you spend copious amounts of time with a person, doing and pursuing things together, you begin to take on some of their characteristics. You pick up many of their habits and ways as these modes of behavior become normal, everyday occurrences to you. Some of these habits are good, such as being on time, exercising, or following a healthier diet. But some of these habits are horrible, like being late, spending money you don't have on things you don't need, or binge-watching Netflix instead of being productive.

While there's a strong possibility bad habits have survived your separation from your ex, there's a near certainty the baggage you brought into the relationship is fully intact. Baggage and bad habits are resilient. A breakup won't shatter them. If cellphone screens were made of our issues and hang ups, we'd never have to repair or replace them!

While they may not look broken, you know your defense mechanisms, destructive thought patterns, and self-destructive behaviors aren't working anymore.

No one wants to be in a relationship with a person who is still in their last relationship. There's nothing more annoying than someone who won't stop comparing you to their ex, or worse, their mother or father. You don't want to be the girl who keeps reliving the same relationship over and over, thinking you can twist your wish list until you discover the combination that unlocks true love and happiness. This system is obviously not working for you. It's time to stop holding on to things that don't work.

People hold on to things that don't work for two reasons: the person who gave it to them or the memories attached to the times it worked. Neither of these reasons are good reasons to hold on to what's not working.

The truth is people you love often give you crappy gifts. Some of these "gifts" are unintentional. Parents try not to pass their worst traits down to their children. They seek to keep their children from experiencing the effects of their upbringing. Yet many fail in this pursuit.

They don't fail because they don't love their children enough. They fail because they don't love themselves enough, they don't pursue healing for themselves, and/or they spend too much time trying to change their habits and not enough changing their hearts.

Most of the people who've damaged us did so because they didn't know who they were or who they belonged to. We must learn to separate who we are at our core from what we do and what has been done to us.

A word of caution: you can't go back to doing everything the way you used to before your relationship. You're not the same person you were before your ex. Don't treat yourself as if you are. It will only lead to disappointment and discouragement when you don't seem to align with yourself.

Instead, as you dig into the sections of this book, evaluate what you think and how you feel **now**. You will notice you're changing as you learn more about yourself and God.

Now that you have some language for some of what's been broken or bruised, let's focus on moving forward.

Breakin' at the Cracks

(Rip)

What is more painful than a breakup?

- Cute stilettos with pointed toes
- Underwire bras, especially when the wire comes out the side and pokes you
- Foot cramps
- Hitting the meaty part of your thigh on a table corner
- A paper cut in the crease of a finger
- Shoes that treat baby toes as expendable appendages
- Walking on a foot that has fallen asleep
- Putting your bra back on to leave your house
- Realizing there's no toilet paper AFTER you've already done your business
- Getting the "bubble guts" when you're nowhere near a respectable bathroom
- Finding store cash/an amazing offer the day AFTER it expires
- When the humidity/wind says, "What great hair day?" and proceeds to disrespect your mane
- Realizing your "fat jeans" are now your everyday jeans
- Waking up exhausted 1-5 minutes before your alarm clock goes off
- When a favorite show is cancelled and ends on a cliff hanger
- When they kill your favorite character off your favorite show
- When game show contestants don't hear you shouting the correct answers and you don't win the money.
- Getting paid on Friday and being broke by Saturday.
- Leaving items in your online cart and paying bills like a grown up.
- Watching videos where 16-year-olds have to name songs from the early 2000s and realizing you're old.

A Clean Break

THE FIRST TIME I EXPERIENCED A BREAK was because of a boy. I was visiting my godmother when it happened. Her brothers and I were playing on her bed. The bed sat high off the ground. It had just the right amount of bounce to the springs to keep a bunch of kids more occupied with jumping on it than watching TV.

I don't know how it started, but we became engrossed in an aggressive game of "tag". The boys kept tagging me and jumping away before I could tag them back. Irritated, I became determined to tackle the next one to hit me.

A boy hit me and jumped to the other side of the bed before I could grab him. He stuck his thumbs in his ears and wiggled his fingers like antlers. He scrunched up his face, stuck out his tongue, and chanted "Na na na na na. You can't get me!"

That was it. He was going down.

I perched along the edge of the bed, my knees and toes digging into the soft mattress as I stared him down. I lined my body up with his position across the bed from me, distributed my weight between my legs and lowered my center of gravity in preparation to pounce. I waited, my body a coil of pent up energy, for him to be lulled into a false sense of security.

The wait was less than ten seconds. In the middle of his finger waving and chanting, I lunged for him. I like to believe my fingertips grazed the material of his shirt as I sailed by, but the exact details are lost in the annals of time. What I do remember is he jumped out of my reach. My forward momentum, without a body to slow it down, propelled me over the side of the bed. I stuck my arm out to stop my fall. My hand drove straight into the floor, the force snapping my forearm. I don't remember if it was the ulna, radius or both. Either way, one mistimed dive meant my right arm was destined to be in a cast for six to eight weeks.

There are few breaks more painful than reaching for something with everything in you and missing. It can leave you unable to catch yourself as you fall headfirst. You may not know when you're going to hit the bottom or how hard the impact is going to be. Every effort you make to prevent the fall could result in further injury. It's difficult to tell if you should try to stop your descent or let gravity take its course.

This is especially true when it comes to breakups. Reaching for a relationship and ending up grasping the wind is a horrible feeling. Equally horrible is falling out of love and into an unknown future without someone you thought would be by your side.

Worse, not all breakups are as clean and clear of a break as my broken arm. One partner might think they are taking a break to "figure things out," while the other person believes the relationship is over for good. Some people are "ghosted" by their partner; their boyfriend or girlfriend disappears without stating the relationship is over. One or both people might want to remain friends, but the reality is different than their intentions.

Often, individuals don't get the opportunity to say what they need to say or ask the questions they want to ask before communication ceases between the parties involved. Even if breaking up is a mutual decision, the people involved may not feel the same way about the breakup or agree on what should happen next. All of this can result in a lack of closure and confusion about what to do next.

When I broke my arm, there was no doubt it was broken. The doctors knew exactly how to proceed with fixing it. That didn't mean they didn't want to investigate the cause. You see, my godmother didn't take me to the hospital when I broke my arm; she took me home. My mother took me to the hospital.

At the hospital, they separated me from my mother and questioned me. How did you get hurt? Who was there? Did your mommy do this? Even though they knew the results, they wanted to know how this had happened and who was at fault.

We can have similar feelings when a relationship ends. We know it's broken, but we become obsessed with the how's and why's. We want to determine fault. How can this be prevented in the future?

We can overthink and overanalyze our breakups. We can also under-analyze the breaks that occur in our lives. It's difficult to find the right balance of understanding and accepting what's happened without obsessing over it.

A book about breakups has to begin with an ending. In this section, we will do just that. You're going to start at the end of the relationship. The following chapters will focus on: what to do immediately following a breakup; understanding and achieving closure, and; praying prayers that change hearts—even broken ones.

You might want to take a deep breath before you turn the page. This is where it gets real.

Case Closed

Did you receive closure after your breakup?

I would say I didn't, just because there weren't really any solid or concrete reasons he had about why we shouldn't continue in our relationship. Our break-up was complicated for a lot of reasons, but I think because it didn't make "sense," that made it even more complicated and difficult.

🖤 Katie H.

I did not receive closure right away but within that next month, I did. It took me a while to grieve, mourn the loss and understand why he did what he did.

🖤 Kacy S.

At the time of the break up, I didn't feel like I had closure. I kept wanting to talk about it with him, but really what we both needed was the space to get over each other. I'm not sure there was much more we needed to discuss. We knew we weren't a good fit, but I feel like I maybe used the idea of closure to keep talking to him. (But I know of others who literally did not get any reasons or answers

after a breakup and in those cases I feel like they really didn't get closure.)
💔 Natalie M.L.

At the immediate time of break up, it felt as if there was closure/peace. About a week or so later, we both were wondering if we made the right decision. We then realized that even though we loved each other, it was not God's plan for us to be together. There wasn't complete closure, but we knew God was saying no.
💔 Ayanna S.

I don't feel I received closure at the time of my last breakup. We officially broke up over text, even though we had had conversations about our relationship in person beforehand. Because I was in college and he was still in high school, we did not see each other for four months after that. I believe God used this time of not having closure or understanding to pull me closer to Him and rely on Him.
💔 Erica U.

The conversation was sudden and completely unexpected. He didn't give much explanation in the moment besides "I don't want to be married anymore," but I oddly felt a peace about the decision immediately. Even though I didn't feel closure yet and didn't even really understand it yet, I knew it was part of the Lord's plan for my life and didn't question it. I rarely feel the Lord speak to me, but he very clearly did in that moment, and said "It's okay. You can go now."
💔 Kelsey B.

Yes, only because my closure was depending upon God. I looked to Him for answers and He gave them to me when I found out about the baby and the multiple affairs. That was all the closure I needed. Through repeated, weekly godly counsel I was able to receive closure in knowing that my ex was not committed to the marriage or me any longer, if he ever was, none of that matter anymore, just my peace.

♥ Cheryl S.

I honestly did not feel closure at the time of the break up. I initially ended it for the purpose of spiritual growth, finding myself, and learning to love myself. I could not for the life of me understand why he no longer wanted to make it work when I went back to revive the relationship.

♥ Andreana J.

Closure can be a mirage ... a shimmering promise of something you crave but won't find if you keep chasing what cannot satisfy.

It is Finished (Isn't It?)

I WAS MOVING INTO MY APARTMENT WHEN I NOTICED IT. Three days after I'd picked up items I had at my ex's place, I realized I had left something. Something marginally important. The remote to my Blu-ray player. Without this remote control, my Blu-ray player was basically inoperable.

I had no intention of ever reaching out to my ex again. His contact information and text string were already erased from my phone. Was it worth it to reach out to him for a remote?

I sent him a quick text to give my remote to a mutual friend when he saw them. After he responded, I deleted the texts and carried on.

I never got my remote back. A couple months later, lightning killed my functioning Blu-ray player but left the remote-less one unharmed. If I was going to watch any of my hundreds of movies, something would have to be done. Was this a sign to reach out to my ex again?

The world will never know, because I didn't reach out to him again. I visited my local big box store and bought a universal remote.

I'm sure my missing remote wasn't a sign from the Lord. I don't think the Lord cares I never got it back. I could have used this minor "crisis" as a convenient excuse to reach out to my ex in the name of "closure," but it wasn't necessary. I had accepted the relationship was over, and there was an alternative that worked for me.

Closure, or lack thereof, can be a big issue immediately following a breakup. Not every relationship is tied up neatly. Some people have legitimate issues they need to resolve with their ex—child visitation schedules, alimony, the division of property, etc. Others are looking for answers they think will provide emotional closure. You may crave a resolution to issues, but one isn't necessary to move on.

When a person breaks something they cherished, they can spend an excessive amount of time pondering if it can be put back together. They examine it from every angle, seeking to understand what's happened and find a way to undo what has been done. They replay the moment it tap-danced off the edge of their fingers in their head on a constant loop. They wish with everything in them that things were different and that they could fix it. But there's no way to rewind the tape. There's no way to undo what's happened. No matter what questions you ask yourself, how much you beat yourself up, or who you allow to berate you or tell you everything you did wrong, it's unlikely these pursuits will give you the closure you so desperately want.

Maybe you think if you knew what went wrong or receive answers to all the questions the relationship left you with, you'll experience this mythical, magical closure. You'll know what to do going forward. Perhaps you believe if you get "justice," if your ex seems to be suffering for the things he's done, you'll feel better. Yet many who have experienced closure and seen the human justice system work in their favor report disappointing results.

You should carefully examine your motivations for wanting closure.

Many of the issues and the work involved in getting over a bad breakup have nothing to do with knowing why your ex did what he did; rather, they hinge on knowing why you responded the way you did. Working through these issues means working on yourself. You need to understand your reactions and motivations. You need to know what influenced you to stay or leave, to run or confront conflict.

You're no longer in a relationship with your ex. While you think it might be useful to understand their reasoning or motivation for their actions, this knowledge isn't necessary for you to move on. We'll discuss what **is** necessary in later sections. For now, suffice it to say closure, at least in the initial stages after a breakup, can be a mirage that keeps you moving in the wrong direction, the shimmering promise of something you crave but won't find if you keep chasing what cannot satisfy.

seeking the Lord,
I ended up
being released from,
letting go of,
and losing my grip on
what wasn't
God's best for me.

Season of Shut Up

I DIDN'T TELL ANYONE I'D BROKEN UP WITH MY EX right away. I waited to share this information, not because I was ashamed or in denial, but because I felt God wanted me to be silent on the matter. I call this period my season of shut up.

In today's world, the majority perspective of having and sharing experiences has shifted. With the explosion of social media and other forms of digital connectivity, the time between having an experience and sharing it with family and friends has decreased so much that in many instances, it's non-existent. Most people make social media posts or even stream experiences as they happen, good or bad. Everything from a man being shot by police to a friend's surprise engagement can pop up in your social media as a live video.

While this connectivity can be a great tool, I've seen many adverse effects result from sharing something without having time to process the experience. People are no longer living in the moment or taking the time to process feelings attached to the moment. They experience the moment through their phone's camera instead of involving all their senses. They don't think about the impact what they're sharing may have on others. They don't consider what would happen if this moment doesn't go as planned. This "live" life leaves no time to make conscious decisions about what to share and what should remain private.

My season of shut up gave me processing time and allowed me to make conscious decisions about what I shared instead of sharing out of raw emotion. This time was crucial in how I was able to shine my light for God's glory in the days, weeks, and months following my breakup. The lack of this time might have stunted what God grew in me during this season.

There are several reasons a person may be in a season where they don't share specific details or information about their private life. Here are some of the reasons I believe I was led not to share about my breakup initially. This is not a prescription to follow. You may not be led to remain silent about your breakup. You may choose not to keep as much to yourself or maintain your silence for as long as I did. But affording yourself some processing time between experiencing your breakup and sharing all the details may be one of the things you can do differently to break right.

1. **I avoided cluttering my head with other people's voices.** Because I was silent, I was able to listen. I experienced a quietness during this season that was unusual for me. As someone who uses chatter to cover up nervousness/anxiety or to delay the inevitable, having a dearth of words meant my feelings and thoughts caught up to me. The last thing I needed in such a raw and sensitive time was insensitive advice or opinions. I didn't need someone's well-meaning but ungraceful trampling of my self-esteem or decision-making abilities. I didn't tell anyone about the breakup, and no one gave me platitudes or permissions I didn't need.

2. **The only voice in my head regarding my breakup was the Lord's.** Since I didn't have a head full of other people, I could hear what God was saying. After getting love and relationships so wrong, I was anxious to know what God had to say to me in this season. My word for the year during this season of continuous breaking was "seek," and in each break, I sought to find what God was doing and what He was showing me. By seeking the Lord, I ended up being released from, letting go of, and losing my grip on what wasn't God's best for me. The stripping happened quickly, but the refining process needed that season of shut up to burn out the impurities. And burn it did!

In my season of shut up, I sat in service, Sunday school, and bible study being served some hard teachings. I turned on podcasts for a pick me up and got hit with humbling truths. I couldn't escape. I thought God would be a Comforter during this time, but instead He was the Truth. His word was indeed sharper than a two-edged sword, and I got cut more than once.

If I had shared my breakup before processing these truths, my story would be very different. It would be filled with feelings, excuses, and hiding places. Some people may have felt they couldn't tell me the truth about myself because I was already hurt. They would co-sign my mess and resolve to tell me about myself later. I might have rejected the truth from people who tried to correct me because I was too busy defending myself and my pain to listen. But when the only perfect God hits you with truth, all you can say is "ouch."

3. **The refining process, to outsiders, can look like crazy on an ordinary day.** Being refined by God looked just as messy, hard and like something only a mother could love as you'd imagine.

By not sharing, I had the opportunity to put things into perspective and order.

Sometimes when you know you have people coming over, instead of organizing and putting your belongings where they go, you just stuff everything in the closet or junk drawers. I didn't want to stuff everything God was revealing to me about who I had been and what I had been doing into the closet of my heart. I wanted to carefully consider and place the things I had neglected, things I'd put down but needed to take back up, and things I'd taken up but needed to sit down. I couldn't afford to shove everything in a junk drawer, closet, attic, or crawlspace. I didn't want to bundle it all up and throw it out without examining it.

To be that messy in front of people, especially people I couldn't be certain would receive me in my "hot mess" state and point me to Christ with wisdom, wasn't going to happen.

4. **People didn't know me and didn't know how to help me.** This realization was part of discovering my true identity after my breakup. I needed to be certain of who I was before I invited others into my space. I knew if I didn't know who I was, others were eager to ascribe an identity to me. The way people translated my actions in the past revealed they didn't understand who I was at my core. They knew things about me, but they didn't know me. Many persisted in seeing me as the same girl or woman they'd met however many years ago and didn't allow their view of me to grow with my personal growth.

People also didn't know me because I didn't know myself. God was changing some things in my heart, and my reactions to what God was doing changed me further. I knew better than to expect other people to know me when I was still being shown things about myself and trying to let God tell me who He created me to be.

Sometimes what God tells you to do won't make sense. People in your life may unknowingly push against His will. They may cause you to question if you heard God right. They don't know God's plans for you, but they may rush in to "fix" the situation or give you "perspective" because they love you and want to help.

When I did tell people about the breakup, I realized they wouldn't have known how to help me. My aunt was upset I didn't tell her. "You've been going through all this alone!" She had wanted to be there for me. The thing is, she was. I came down to visit her during my season of shut up for nearly a week. That time was restorative for me. I didn't need to talk about the breakup, cry or get angry for her to help me through it.

Others I told responded with disparaging remarks about my ex or my relationship, encouraged me to go out and meet someone new, or offered a shoulder to cry on that I didn't need. God had already established something He was working on with me. He'd given me something to do. Finding another man would only serve to help me bury all the things I didn't want to deal with under the foundation of a new relationship. But my family and friends didn't get that because they didn't know how God had changed me.

5. **It allowed me to be more than someone who had just experienced a breakup.** I didn't have to deal with everyone asking "How are you holding up? Is everything OK?" right after my breakup. I didn't have to suffer through awkward conversations where people tried to avoid mentioning my ex or watched what they said to avoid bringing up my recent heartache. I had time to fortify myself before dealing with

people who would ride roughshod over my feelings as they attempted to extract every detail they could about the breakup.

I focused on serving others during this time. I went to the homes of sick church members after service and worshiped with them. I fellowshipped with members of my church family over meals after service. I helped prepare for events. Those times are precious to me. I needed to get outside of myself and my situation. I needed to make my world bigger than my breakup again. Serving allowed me to do this. Being silent about my recent split meant no one felt they needed to tend to me as I tended to others. I was able to be of service instead of people feeling they should serve me. I got to be more than the girl who'd just ended a relationship.

6. **I had the chance to be sad.** Sometimes a breakup isn't real to you directly after it happens. It's easy to pronounce yourself as fine when your reality hasn't hit home yet. Conversely, you might be devastated after your breakup, but with time and space to process the experience before sharing it, you have come to accept ending the relationship was the right decision regardless of who made it.

I don't think people realize how much pressure one can feel not to be sad when they tell others about their breakup. You may feel you have to say "no, I'm fine. Don't worry about me." You don't want anyone to change their life to come see about you.

Many women feel as if they always have to be OK. They deny their feelings because they don't have time or permission to be sad. Maybe you have a child or other responsibilities that require you to keep it together. You can't call in sick or take a mental health day from everyone and everything that needs your attention, even when you just want an afternoon to eat ice cream and binge Netflix in stretchy pants and a t-shirt.

I realize having a season of shut up as long as mine was isn't common or even possible for many women. Even if all you can manage is a few hours, an afternoon or a weekend, I encourage you to take some time out to process what's happened before cluttering your heart with other people's opinions and perspectives. Take the time to pray, cry, journal, clean, make homemade bread, go for a run, or hit the gym.

Later, I'll share how and what I told people about my break up, but for right now, I want you to take a deep breath. That breath may hitch in your chest or throat. It might turn into a sigh or a sob. That's OK. You don't have to be superwoman and leap over sadness or conflicting emotions in a single bound for me. You don't have to be sad or feel bad if the only things you feel right now are peace and freedom. Feel whatever it is. Pick it up and examine it. Set it before God and ask Him what it means. God will give you wisdom without ridiculing you for not already knowing everything.

Whether you take seconds or a season to process what's happened and determine how you want to move forward, my encouragement to you is to involve God in this process. Don't shut Him out or drown His voice out with the voices of others. God is near and ready to bind up your wounds. He wants to begin restoring you.

Maybe, however unintentionally, you locked Him out of your relationship. Maybe the failure of your relationship has you angry with Him or unwilling to trust Him. Maybe you drifted far away from Him without realizing it. Sometimes we can become so wrapped up in what's going on in our lives that we lose sight of eternity.

If any of this resonates with you, get before the Lord. It's OK to pour it all out, to tell Him everything you're feeling or worried about not feeling. That's a good step.

But at some point, Sister, you need to shut up. Sit silently before the Lord. Open your heart and your bible and LISTEN. Don't listen to respond in defense of your position; listen to His lovingkindness. Listen for His leading. Listen to learn He never left you alone. If you've left Him, draw near to Him; He'll draw near to you in turn. Cry if you have to. Repent if you need to. But please, with all due respect, SHUT UP and LISTEN.

SEASON OF SHUT UP SURVIVAL KIT

Every season of life needs a survival kit, tools and tricks we can employ to help us survive and even thrive as we're walking through it. My season of shut up was no different. As someone who processes through words, not being able to verbalize what I was experiencing proved to be difficult. I needed to acquire tools and implement structures to assist me in making the most of this season.

I've taken the time to list a few of the more useful tools in my season of shut up survival kit below. I've continued to use many of them in my current season. These tools worked for me, but feel free to adjust them to suit your specific season and situation. Utilize what works with your personality and the goals you want to achieve. I pray some or all of these resources can be useful to you as you navigate the season you're in.

💔 SUPPLIES

- **BIBLE**: This is a given in any season I'm in. If I don't have my bible, I'm not equipped to handle anything. The bible is my go to guide and contains everything I need pertaining to life and godliness.

It's bread and water, comfort and encouragement, conviction and command, and all-consuming love. I can't survive without it.

- **PRAYER**: Since God was the only one I could tell about what I was going through, prayer became another lifeline for me. It's one of the few places I could pour out and share EVERYTHING I was feeling. It continues to be a safe place to be honest and vulnerable. I go into more detail about my prayer life after my breakup in "Prayer: Not for the Petty of Heart," but suffice it to say prayer became a release, recharge, and reset in my life like never before during this season.

- **JOURNALING**: I've kept a diary or journal since the third grade. While the musings of baby Erica can be painful to read today, I treasure those early journals. It's easy to see my growth, track patterns, and find encouragement in reading what I've lived through. Journaling isn't just therapeutic; it gives me an accurate record I can analyze and learn from. Seeing what I've come through gives me courage and reassures me I'll make it through my present storms. My journals remind me of scriptures I've studied that apply to my current situation. They help me remember when I struggled with certain sins and weights. They make me more sympathetic and gracious toward those currently struggling with the same things.

- **MUSIC**: Music speaks to me on an emotional level. As the stepdaughter of a jazz musician who comes from a family of singers, I grew up surrounded by music. My writing and speech have always been influenced and informed by sound. When I'm hurting, there's nothing like pouring out in song. Singing is different than praying. Many songwriters give language to emotions many of us feel but can't communicate with words. In my season of shut up, feel good, encouraging music was my go to mood lifter.

- **LONG WALK**: When I'm trying to work through things, my mouth isn't the only thing that wants to move. I walk. It's my way of getting excess energy out. It's something to do other than being cooped up in the house. When I walk, I listen to music/podcasts, pray, and brainstorm books and blogs. Sometimes I just walk, listening to birds or traffic and feeling the sun on my arms. Either way, it calms me and forces my mind to slow down.

- **MOVIES**. I LOVE movies. I have a full DVD wall rack filled with various genres. Movies and books are my escapes. Not every moment needs to be spent doing deep soul work or pouring out emotion. Sometimes I want to get lost in what's going on in someone else's life—even if that personal is fictional.

- **BOOKS.** Books have been crucial to all the seasons of my life. I read to learn, to be entertained, and to pass the time in waiting rooms. In my season of shut up, I read several amazing books that shifted my perspective, as well as great books that provided a reprieve from the stresses of life.

- **SERVING OTHERS.** Having something constructive to do that took me outside of myself was invaluable to me while going through my season of shut up. I already mentioned visiting and having worship service with the sick, but there were other ways I served others during this time. I took a friend's maternity photos. I helped plan and organize a family Christmas party. I accompanied a group of young ladies to the Christian bookstore and educated them on bible translations, studies, and reference materials. Serving others, instead of emptying me, filled me up.

♥ TOOLS/SEASON HACKS

- **Manage social media instead of being managed by social media.** I changed the way I interacted with social media, and it did wonders to change my mindset during this season. I changed both what I was putting out and what I was taking in. I filled my timeline with people who posted and shared stories and pictures reflective of the perspective I wanted to have moving forward. I unfollowed and unfriended people full of negativity. I speak about the reasons for reevaluating my social media in "Shut Up on Social Media" and "Stop Stalking on Social Media."

- **Routine answers to questions about my relationship.** When people asked me about my ex or my relationship in this season, I had specific responses I decided on in advance. If someone asked where he was, I would be honest and say I didn't know. If they asked why they hadn't seen him lately, I would encourage them to contact him for themselves. If anyone asked about my relationship, which they did not, I had an answer for that as well. I also used redirection. Having an honest, preselected answer made me more comfortable going into social situations. I didn't have to hide out to keep from sharing before I should, neither was I caught unawares and scrambling for an answer.

SHUTTING UP ON SOCIAL MEDIA

Social media is a tool. Whether it's a tool for the devil or the Lord is up to you. Your social media, like most areas of your life, is a battlefield, a place where war is waged to see who will be defeated and who will get the glory.

We are at war in a breakup. It may feel as if you've already lost the war. You've lost the relationship. You've lost the person. You lost the future you saw for yourself, and you feel like all is lost.

But sweetheart, that's just one battle, one skirmish in a very long war. You have a unique opportunity to gain a foothold and an advantage in this war by how you proceed in the battles that come after the "defeat" of a breakup. One of those battlefields or battlegrounds is our social media.

You control the valve that determines the flow of information and content. You don't have to share everything. You control what you share with people online as well as in real life (IRL). Be strategic and intentional about it. Adjust the flow as you see fit.

If you feel like too much is being shared too fast, scale back. Don't be intimidated into oversharing. Don't let what people might think or say keep you from posting what God places on your heart. If you want to post something about your breakup that you've prayed over, searched the scriptures concerning, and sought wise counsel on, don't be shamed into not posting it.

Here are a few tips to use social media effectively after a breakup, especially in a season of shut up:

💔 THINK BEFORE YOU POST:

Ask yourself the following questions before you post about your ex or your relationship to social media:

- Is this something someone needs to know?
- Can someone see the Lord in this or be encouraged by this?
- Does this reveal an essential truth about who God is?
- Does this post place blame?
- Am I posting this to gain approval, "win" people to my side, or manipulate feelings and sympathies?
- Am I using this platform to share the goodness of the Lord, even in this situation, or am I stirring up and

rallying the troops to fight the wrong war?

❤ CONSIDER JESUS

Before posting to social media or blogs, consider Jesus. Consider His death, burial, and resurrection to afford you the opportunity of salvation. Consider the goodness of God to you when you've been way less than good to Him. Consider how God feels about your ex and how God would feel about what you're saying. Then decide if you still want to publish the post.

❤ FOREGO FALSE FRONTS

Check your social media to ensure you're not putting up a false front. Yes, social media is a curated representation of our lives, but if we're going to show the goodness of God even in a bad situation, then we need to use social media intentionally, prayerfully, and strategically. We need to share some of what we are struggling with or learning. We need to reveal how we're applying the things we're learning.

❤ SHARE WHAT YOU LEARN

Whether you're in a season of shut up, sharing everything, or somewhere in between, it's possible to share what you're learning and experiencing in a way that is both authentic and shines your light. Here are a few tips for curating a feed that does this:

- If you're in a season of shut up, share what you're learning and experiencing without referencing your breakup.
- Post on topics without referencing your relationship.
- Share what God is teaching you through your study of His word or prayer.

❤️ SET BOUNDARIES AND STICK TO THEM

Posting anything about your relationship ending can open the floodgates in your comments section. People may push for details you don't want to give. They may try to bully you with reminders of how much you shared and posted when you were in love and demand you post what happened to break you up. They might claim an investment in your relationship because of perceived oversharing.

Don't be intimidated by this. Don't be spurred into saying something you might regret. You don't have to answer or address such inquiries. Everyone is entitled to their opinion, not your attention or explanation.

❤️ STAND FIRM AND BLOCK

When you post, use discernment and be led by the Holy Spirit. Speak the truth in love. Post only what you're willing to stand behind. Don't get into back and forth arguments with people about what you post. Delete comments that are abusive or offensive. Block people who viciously attack you in comments on your posts or in your direct messages.

❤️ WATCH YOUR WORDS

As a Christian, you have a responsibility to watch your words wherever your words are heard, read or seen. Set a guard over your heart, mouth, ears, and eyes. Be intentional about what goes into your heart, because out of the abundance the heart, the mouth speaks (and fingers post!).

Don't allow roots of bitterness to grow unchecked because of who may or may not be able to see what you say on social media. Don't use your social media to spread gossip. Don't block your ex to prevent them from seeing the mean-spirited things you post about them. Don't use your social media to spread lies or bitterness. The bible says liars, and other immoral, sinful people will be thrown into the lake of fire, which is the second death, at the judgment (Rev. 21:8). You will have to give an account of every careless word you speak (Matt. 12:36). Bashing your ex isn't worth the weeping and gnashing of teeth that can result when we refuse to make our speech submit to the word of God.

EXITING A SEASON OF SHUT UP

I didn't have a plan for exiting my season of shut up. I figured I would know when the time was right to start sharing news of my breakup with those close to me. I knew why I wasn't sharing, and I believed I would know why I was sharing it when the time came.

There are times when you need to exit a season of shut up immediately and share what's going on with someone equipped to help you. If you find that you're in a depressed state, engaging in self-destructive behaviors, or are more emotionally impacted than you're able to cope with alone, exit this season IMMEDIATELY. It's one thing to feel the need to verbally process things with a friend when you know God wants you to sit in this with Him; it's another when you're having suicidal thoughts. You need to share this with someone who can get you help.

Furthermore, if you find not talking about your breakup is your way of avoiding acknowledging and dealing with what's happened, it's time to speak up. My season of shut up wasn't about an unwillingness to accept my relationship was over. It was a time set apart to seek the Lord, to depend on and reconnect with Him. It was time to work through what happened, not to avoid it or run from it.

If emotional struggles aren't forcing you out of your season of shut up, how do you know it's time to exit this season?

For me, I knew I was ready to exit this season when I felt ready to receive the commentary I knew I would receive. I knew people would have opinions and questions, but I wouldn't be swayed one way or another by those observations.

I also knew it was time to share because I was receiving inquiries about my ex's whereabouts or life that I couldn't answer. During my season of shut up, I pointed these people to my ex and encouraged them to reach out to him. When someone asked where he was, and I felt peace about sharing the breakup with them, I did.

I thought I would know what to say when the time came to say it. How hard could it be to state the fact I'm no longer in a relationship with someone, especially after taking the time to process the pain of the breakup? As prepared as I was, people still made comments or asked questions I didn't know how to respond to or address. Some of their comments were rude or judgmental. Some meant well, but their opinions weren't helpful.

When you announce your breakup, be prepared to hear everything anyone ever wanted to say about you and your ex's relationship. The things people felt "released" to share after my breakup were eye opening. But the season I spent processing the breakup with God gave me an inner strength I didn't know I had. I was able to stick with what I wanted to say. I didn't let people goad me into saying things I would regret or beat myself up about sharing with them.

The tips I share won't cover every possible response you will receive. Some responses will have you itching to explain or defend yourself, your ex, or your relationship. Don't let what you hear determine what you say. Remember, you set the boundaries.

Without further ado, here are a few tips and considerations for exiting your season of shut up:

- **You don't have to share with everyone at the same time.** You don't have to put it on social media or share it with people you aren't close to at the same time you tell your inner circle.
- **You don't have to share everything with everyone.** There will be layers to sharing your breakup. You may choose not to tell your grandmother and your girlfriends the same things about your breakup. You can choose to tell some people you broke up without offering an explanation. You might tell associates the main thing, close friends the important things, and a counselor everything (or your mother. That's cool, too).
- **You don't owe anyone an explanation for your breakup.** If you don't feel compelled to give an explanation to an individual, don't. Don't let anyone force you into divulging details you're uncomfortable with them knowing. There's nothing wrong with saying "I prefer to keep the details private."
- **You don't have to share with everyone at the same time.** The first person I told was a close friend I knew wouldn't gossip about what I shared with her. I shared on a person by person basis as I felt comfortable. The last place I shared the information was on social media. Determine how you want to dispense information before you start telling people. Whether you want to "get it over with" and state it on social media, or tell the people closest to you first, do what works for you.
- **Be intentional about who you choose to tell first, second, and third.** If you choose the gradual approach, the best people to tell first are people you can trust not to spread your business. You may require someone with a level of expertise and experience dealing with specific issues you're facing. Those required to keep your conversations confidential by HIPPA laws, such as licensed counselors, and those bound by spiritual conviction,

like ministers, elders, and strong believers, should be strongly considered as first responders. There's nothing worse than hearing details of a private discussion being shared by someone you didn't include in that vulnerable conversation.

You want the first reactions you get to be from people who love you. It's ideal if those individuals can tell you the truth in love. When I exited my season of shut up, I wanted the first people I told to be people who could stand in love and gently but firmly tell me the truth. These were women and men who knew God intimately, who could remind me of who I was and to whom I belonged. I needed strong Christians around me who wouldn't engage in pettiness with me or encourage behaviors that weren't reflective of who I was in Christ. I needed truth poured into me, and the people I surrounded myself with didn't withhold it from me. I urge you to choose people who know God intimately and can say to you "This is who your Father is. This is who Jesus is. This is who the Comforter is. And this is who He made you to be."

With the click of a few keys, I can access hordes of people willing to tell me I did everything right and everything that went wrong was my ex's fault. There are plenty of forums where women complain about men being dogs, pigs, and other farm animals. But I didn't need these lies putting down roots and growing in my heart.

A broken heart is fertile, freshly tilled soil; whatever you plant in it has the potential to yield a huge crop in your life. Don't plant seeds of bitterness in this season. Seek to sow and grow fruit you will be excited to harvest in due season.

Stop Stalking Your Ex on Social Media

SOCIAL MEDIA HAS CHANGED THE LANDSCAPE of dating and relationships. Not only has social media provided more ways to connect with the people already in our lives, it has given people we don't know unprecedented access to information about our lives. Many relationships start and play out on social media. Unfortunately, so do breakups.

When you break up with someone, social media can become a minefield. Time Hop and "On This Day" features dredge up pictures and posts from happier, coupled up times. Posts by mutual friends containing subliminal messages about your breakup might end up in your newsfeed. One of the most devastating and quickly executed emotional moments can occur when a relationship status is changed from "in a relationship" to "single."

What we share on social media is important, but you also need to consider what you consume from social media. As I stated before, social media is a tool. It can be used to help you or hurt you. It's up to you to evaluate its usefulness to you in this season. Consider what you consume and make educated decisions on your social media diet.

There are a few possible approaches to addressing social media consumption during a breakup:

💔 **FAST FROM SOCIAL MEDIA.** You may want to fast from social media altogether for a period after your breakup. You can delete the apps from your phone, block the sites on your computer or deactivate your social media accounts. The **length** of your fast should be determined by the **purpose** of your fast. Don't break your fast until you have accomplished the goals you set for it, whether the goal is a certain amount of time, an answer to a specific prayer, after a certain event occurs, etc.

Life will go on. People will continue to post the profound, the silly, the educational, and the fantastical. You won't miss much. The goal is to return with a fresh perspective and renewed mindset.

💔 **POLICE YOUR PAGES.** When you're trying to achieve closure, you may have to close off all avenues by which information about your ex or memories of the relationship can get to you. Fasting isn't the only option you have to achieve this goal. If you don't want to fast from social media, or are returning after a fast, you can take advantage of several advancements in social media which allow you to tailor your feeds in ways that work for you.

When I changed my relationship status on Facebook from "in a relationship with" to "single," a message popped up. This message said Facebook noticed my change in relationship status. It then listed several options I could use to control everything from whether I wanted to see posts involving my ex in my memories to what posts I would see from my ex going forward, all in one convenient place. You can erase an ex from your Facebook memories much more effectively than the old school solution of cutting them out of pictures.

There are other advances in social media you can use to your advantage during a breakup. You can unfollow, unfriend, block, or mute people or hashtags. You can mute them for specific periods of time or forever. This is one situation in which social media's many algorithms and automations can work for you.

❤ **One approach to addressing social media that should NEVER be an option is stalking your ex's social media.** This approach benefits no one. It's not constructive to lurk on your ex's pages to see if he is dating anyone or missing you. It's not cool to click through his friends' pages to see if they mention him. If your relationship is truly over, let. It. Go.

❤ **PROTECT YOUR PEACE.** Seeing and receiving input from social media can foster anger, resentment, and bitterness. This bitterness might come from following your ex, mutual friends, or hashtags. Like many other aspects of a breakup, this is one where you need to exercise discernment. You might need to stop following #engaged for a season. You might want to unfriend your ex on social media. That "messy" friend who will attempt to engage you with petty gossip about your ex's new girlfriend? Mute, unfollow or unfriend him or her. Some friends will need to be "unfriended" in real life as well as on social media. Do what you have to do to protect your peace and allow space for healing.

The *mouth speaks* what the *heart's full of.* Consider before you *consume.* Don't let *social media* consume you.

Prayer: Not for the Petty of Heart

IMAGINE THIS: you recently experienced a breakup, but you aren't acting like you're broken. You aren't behaving like a typical crazy ex-girlfriend. Instead of speaking in a derogatory way about your ex or demeaning their character on social media as expected, you speak well of them or not at all. Instead of behaving badly to get your ex's attention, you're pressing in to your relationship with Christ and being content with where He has you. You're acting like a spiritually and emotionally whole person who isn't bowing down, chained up, or enslaved to what was done to you. You aren't bound by an "eye for an eye" mentality. You aren't telling your first dates all the sordid details of your last relationship. You've moved on in a healthy way that shows who you serve.

When others see you behaving this way, it creates an opportunity for you to witness to them about Jesus. If your ex is an unbeliever, your treatment of him post-breakup is a bigger testimony to what you truly believe and where you really place your hope than anything that happened in the relationship. If your ex is a believer, He sees how God is working in you and pushes himself to get closer to the Lord. God is getting glory out of what promised to be a situation without a redeeming facet.

Most of us don't wake up one day with the ability to shine our light as brightly for Christ after a breakup as the person in the above scenario. We're doing well to speak civilly to our ex at church or during awkward run-ins at the local department store. No, this sort of attitude and behavior isn't bestowed on most of us; it's the hard fought for fruit of hours spent in prayer to the Father.

Prayer will shift your focus. It will cause you to behave differently than those in the world going through the same experience. Praying for your ex can mark the beginning of moving on and cultivating an attitude of acceptance and peace. It's the first step away from "crazy ex" territory and toward "Christian who actually behaves like a Christ follower." If you cannot pray for, live peaceably among, and do good to all men, including your ex, then it's time to grow in God and do what He's commanded expressly in His word.

There's something I can't help but add here. Not every person who avoids praying for their ex does so because they don't believe prayer changes things; rather, some avoid it because they **know** prayer changes hearts. They aren't sure they want how they feel about their ex to change. They don't know what they might feel or where those feelings might lead. They ask, "If I surrender my heart to God's will, what will He require of me?"

In my experience with praying for my ex, I learned the Lord required three things of me: love, reconciliation, and forgiveness.

♥ LOVE

When I pray for people, it changes my heart toward them. I become invested in their wellbeing and success. I look for things to pray for on their behalf. I begin to love them in a deeper, more Christ-like way, even my ex.

Putting "love" and "ex" in the same sentence used to make me cringe. The whole "in a Christ-like way" monkey wouldn't stop my shudder show. I didn't want to love my ex. But what did God want me to do?

Maybe the thought of loving your ex makes you cringe, too. Maybe you're trying to fall out of love with your ex. If you know the power of prayer, you may be reticent to pray for someone who hurt you, lied to you, cheated on you, stole from you, etc., whether physically, spiritually or emotionally. You aren't really into this "love the sinner, hate the sin" mentality. You might be scared if you love them "in a totally Christ-like way," those romantic feelings might slip back in, and you won't fully heal and move on.

I could write a whole book on why you need to forgive your ex to move on. This book includes a whole chapter on forgiveness. Most people would agree with the need to forgive their ex even if they didn't want to do it. They can handle extending forgiveness, for themselves if not for their ex. Encouraging you to love your ex, however, is a different thing altogether.

But what does the bible say?

> If anyone says, "I love God," and hates his brother, he is a liar; for he who does not love his brother whom he has seen cannot love God whom he has not seen. 1 John 4:20

Love is where forgetful forgiveness comes from—it keeps no record of wrongs (1 Cor. 13:5 NIV). Love is longsuffering (1 Cor. 13:4). You know, like how God is longsuffering, not willing that any should perish but that all should come to repentance (2 Pet. 3:9)? All includes your ex.

When I came to this realization, I didn't like it either. I didn't have a problem thinking of my prayers heaping coals of fire on my ex's head (Prov. 25:21-22; Rom. 12:19-20). It didn't bother me to classify him as someone I "have to" pray for and forgive. I respect his right to live, breathe clean air and be free from unlawful imprisonment. But love?

If your ex is a Christian, you are commanded to love them. Jesus states that the greatest commandment is to love the Lord and the second is to love your neighbor as yourself (Matt. 22:36-40). The whole of the law can be summed up in these two commandments. Jesus also said, "A new commandment I give to you, that you love one another. By this all people will know you are my disciples, if you have love for one another (John 13:34-35)." People will identify us as Christ followers by how we love each other.

John takes it even further:

> 7 Beloved, let us love one another, for love is from God,
> and whoever loves has been born of God and knows God.
> 8 Anyone who does not love does not know God, because
> God is love. 1 John 4:7-8

Loving one another shows that we know God and are His children.

When we read the often-quoted verses in 1 Corinthians 13 describing the characteristics of love in light of John's assertion that God is love, it changes everything. If we don't have love, none of what we say, do, or have matters.

This knowledge further sharpens the connection between love and forgiveness. Love "keeps no record of wrongs" and "covers a multitude of sin." If we are to imitate Christ and strive to be children of God, we must strive for the same to be said of us in every situation. We should strive to embody love, even toward our exes.

❤ RECONCILIATION

God wants you to love your ex, but what about liking them? For some reason, I thought I could love someone I no longer liked. I thought "I love him, but I don't like him" was completely valid. But through studying the Word and prayer, I learned I couldn't hang on to this attitude if I was going to love, and forgive, like Jesus. If I was going to be like Jesus, I had to learn the ministry of reconciliation.

Reconciliation is a big theme in the bible. It is the puzzle piece that connects love and forgiveness. Every definition of reconciliation can be boiled down to harmony. Reconciliation is the restoring of friendly relations, to make compatible, to make consistent. Unity is the point of reconciliation. Paul continually mentions the unity to be found in Christ: "There is one body and one spirit... one Lord, one faith, one baptism, one God and Father of all who is over all and through all and in all (Eph. 4:4-6)" "...for you are all one in Christ Jesus (Gal. 3:28b)." We are all part of the body of Christ. How can you be one with a part of the body you don't like?

If not for the ministry of reconciliation spoken of in II Cor. 5:18-6:13, which talks about Christ taking on our sin so through Him we might become the righteousness of God, we wouldn't have the hope of eternal life.

Paul describes his work and the work of others in the ministry of reconciliation as putting no stumbling blocks in anyone's way. He talks about being commended by hardships, fruits of the spirit, and the power of God. Finally, he describes the hearts of himself and his co-laborers in the faith as "wide open." There is no limit to their affection for the believers at Corinth. He speaks to them and tells them to widen their hearts as well. Hearts wide open is a requirement for reconciliation. We can't have closed off hearts and serve the way Paul describes in this passage of scripture and several others.

❣ FORGIVENESS

The third and final piece of this puzzle is forgiveness. The definition Minister Harvey Drummer, Jr. gives for forgiveness is to act as if the offense never occurred. A biblical picture of forgiveness is found in Psalm 103:12: as far as the east is from the west, so far does he remove our transgressions from us.

If Christ is our example in all things, we need to ask ourselves "What is Jesus' attitude/stance on forgiveness? What does He expect from me when dealing with my ex after the personal connection has been severed?"

Christ taught forgiveness. The apostles and writers of the New Testament taught forgiveness. Forgiveness is an important component of our walk with the Lord. Forgiveness is what facilitates reconciliation. Forgiveness makes restoring friendly relations and achieving compatibility possible. Forgiveness is one of the things you are called to as a Christian:

> [32] And be ye kind one to another, tenderhearted, forgiving one another, even as God for Christ's sake hath forgiven you. Eph. 4:32

Why do we need to talk about forgiveness when we talk about prayer? When Jesus gave The Sermon on the Mount, He taught the people how to pray. In the Lord's Prayer, Jesus instructs the people to pray to God "And forgive us our debts, as we forgive our debtors (Matt. 6:12)." Jesus emphasizes this point by stating if we don't forgive, we won't be forgiven (Matt. 6:14-15).

Everything I've ever experienced has proven the need for genuine forgiveness, especially if your ex is in the household of faith. Even if they're not, you are called to do good toward them and to pray for them. This is not to heap coals of fire on their heads or bring judgment on them. It is to be done with a pure heart toward them.

Make no mistake: it's going to be difficult to pray for someone you feel has hurt you or tossed you aside. It's hard to pray for someone you know isn't praying for you or wishing you well. It's an exercise in humility to pray contentment for someone you don't believe wants to see you happy. But you can't operate in your flesh or get stuck on how you feel. You can't cast aside what God expects in favor of how you feel in the moment or what someone "deserves."

No one gets what they really deserve, especially Christians. God gave the best for a people who could offer Him nothing in return but continuously falling short. When you were lost and helpless, God prepared and offered a sacrifice to satisfy His righteousness and provide you with the opportunity to be saved. The bible says while we were still sinners, Christ died for us (Rom. 5:8). Even when you took your time coming to God, He was long suffering, not willing that you should perish.

I get it. Elevating your conversation about your ex to a level where it's circumspect and in line with what God wants for them might feel like the emotional equivalent of herding cats right now. Maybe you can't imagine there will ever be a time when you can pray for your ex to be blessed with any authenticity. Praying for them is equivalent to a pageant prayer: you know what you've been coached to say, but you don't feel free to state your real opinion. Not if you want to "win" at being a good Christian.

Prayer wasn't given to man for man to impress God with how pretty he could pray. God doesn't need your prayers to have alliteration, rhyme schemes, or bullet points. He wants you to come boldly and make your requests and petitions known. He wants you to cry out to Him with the belief He can do the thing you desperately need Him to do. He wants you to pour out to Him. And sometimes being honest and sincere in prayer isn't pretty. It's downright ugly. The kind of ugly only your Heavenly Father could love.

THINGS I PRAYED FOR MY EX

I decided early on after I broke up with my ex to pray for him. I prayed for him more after we broke up than I did when we were together. I prayed his relationship with God would remain strong. I prayed he would find a church where he could grow into the man God wanted him to be. I prayed he would remain sensitive to the things God placed on his heart. I prayed he would grow in his career. In short, I prayed the things I'd been praying on his behalf long before we'd broken up.

When you're in an intimate relationship with someone, you know what's closest to their heart. You know what they need, what they lack, and what they want. You've seen where they are weak. You know what they hope for and what has hurt them. Who better to petition the Father for these things on their behalf?

Prayer is a constructive use of your knowledge of your ex. Chances are you pray for people you don't know by name without being privy to the specifics of their situations every day: victims of natural disasters, terrorist attacks, or mass shootings; Christians being persecuted for their beliefs; homeless people you pass on your way to work, etc. Those prayers aren't any less effective because you don't know the details. But you do know some of the specifics of what your ex may need, and as a Christian, you should pray for them.

This isn't an excuse to keep tabs on them. You don't need to check their social media or call their mother to see how they're doing so you can pray for them. You don't have to talk to mutual friends to find out what's going on with them to make your prayers more accurate.

Sometimes fresh details are tools of the enemy to disrupt your peace. They can hurt you, make you jealous, or plant sinful seeds in your heart. Don't disrupt your peace, but pray for your ex. Take your emotional temperature with prayer. Examining what you can honestly pray for your ex will show you areas where the break has been repaired and areas still being knit together.

If you find out your ex has a new person in their life, you can pray for them as well. If the person isn't a Christian, you can pray they become obedient to the call of Christ. If the person is a Christian, you can pray their faith and relationship with Christ is strengthened, that they will model their life after Jesus. If you know specifics, you can pray about them. The choice is yours.

BUT I DON'T FEEL LIKE IT

Don't think this is something I've perfected. I don't always have a handle on it. If you can't imagine yourself being able to do this, I can relate. I've felt that way myself. I don't have this down, but the one thing that's helped me the most to get better at this is learning to pray honestly.

Honesty is one of the most important privileges we can exercise as a Christian. It's also one of the most underutilized tools in a Christian's toolbox. You have permission to be completely honest with God about how you feel.

Some people fake "fine." They pretend as if everything is fine. They pray without being 100% honest. They pray their ex remains a Christian and God still works in his life without addressing their feelings. They will never say "This really sucks. I have complicated feelings about this person, the way things happened and/or how we broke up. I didn't get the closure I wanted. This doesn't feel closed.

It feels raw and open."

They won't admit when they see their ex it feels like someone is stabbing them in the chest with a rusty blade. They won't acknowledge the fact they avoid certain songs, TV shows or movie franchises because those things remind them of times they shared with their ex. They won't confront the fact that when something happens to them, they pick up the phone to call their ex before they remember they don't have a relationship with him anymore.

One of the main reasons people can't be honest about their feelings is because they won't be honest about their faults. People who've built their identity, schedules, and/or happiness around a title or a position may feel lost when the connection is severed. Many will bury their feelings or pretend they don't exist instead of admitting they built their hopes on things that weren't eternal.

When you build integral parts of your life on something or someone and find it isn't as stable a foundation as you believed, don't be too embarrassed to collect your valuables and move out. As someone who has suffered a lot in life unnecessarily because I refused to look stupid, I can attest to the fact saving face isn't worth the price you pay.

I prayed about my feelings concerning my ex, our relationship, and things I've learned about our relationship since we broke up. I prayed about the good, bad, and ugly. I prayed to reconcile what happened in our relationship, to learn and heal from it. I laid everything at Jesus' feet and left it there.

Once I began to pray honestly about my feelings, I noticed there wasn't as much tension between praying for my ex and praying authentically as I once believed. Praying for my ex forced me to work past bitterness and ill will, things I didn't realize I felt until I prayed for him. The Word of God exposes what's in your heart. Repentance and confession are necessary for the forgiveness of all the sin you see in the light of the Word.

If you can't offer up an honest and sincere prayer for your ex, you're not prepared to begin a relationship with anyone else. If you can't pray someone is successful when you're not a part of their lives, you have a much more pressing issue than who will be your spouse. You are in a struggle with selfishness, pride, or a lack of humility. This needs to be addressed before you attempt to attach yourself to another flawed human being.

WHAT I DIDN'T PRAY FOR MY EX

One of the questions I try to ask myself frequently about my prayer life is "What can't I say and mean in prayer?" It doesn't matter if what I can't say is about my ex, my breakup or any other break I've experienced. Where do I feel I can't go in prayer? Why can't I go there?

I don't beat myself up about what I discover. I'm honest with myself and God. I reward that honesty instead of attacking it. I tell God what still feels tender. I ask Him to heal me in that area and take the pain away. I leave room for God to work on that area of my heart and mind. I stop poking it and expecting it not to hurt.

The things you may feel you can't pray about aren't always the same as what you don't pray about. I have never prayed for my ex's current or future relationships. I could, but I don't. I have peace about the relationship ending and I respect his right to move on. But his romantic relationships are as much my concern as any celebrity relationship played out in the tabloids. It would be just as pointless for me to stay "tuned in" and keep up with who he's dating and what they're doing.

Your prayer life may look nothing like mine. Every breakup is different. How you handle your breakup is personal and only needs to work for you. The important thing is to be led by the Lord, not your feelings.

YOU GET WHAT YOU PRAY FOR

When I stopped praying petty prayers, I started praying powerful ones. These powerful prayers didn't originate in my flesh or my feelings, but from the conviction I felt reading and hearing the Word of God. These prayers were my heart's yearnings for the peace and rest God promises in His word.

Powerful prayers confirm you are being who you were created to be, not the identity sticker you stuck on yourself when you were in your relationship. They occur when you acknowledge your true identity is found in Christ. This discovery will make you fight to keep your identity sacred and whole. These are steps on the road back to wholeness.

God answers prayers for me, but not always in the way I want Him to. When you know you'll get what you pray for, you learn to kick cute to the curb and get real with the Lord. You won't waste time praying for what sounds "cool" or "holy." You won't seek after the pat on the back. You will become bold and ask for what you want. Above all, you will pursue God and His will for your life.

My breakup was the answer to a fervent prayer of mine. The answer to a prayer of my heart turned out to be a severed connection and a life repositioning. I won't lie. It hurt not getting the answer I wanted. I prayed with the unspoken expectation things would turn out exactly as I envisioned them: I would get to marry my ex, have my dream career, and stay where I was comfortable. But that wasn't what happened. At. All.

I wasn't expecting God to break things off, but I prayed for Him to do that. I thought I was being super holy when I prayed for Him to take off, take away, and break down anything that wasn't of Him or wasn't pleasing to Him. I was bold enough to tell God to remove it and put it where I had no opportunity to get it back again. I was naïve, but I was also sincere. I wanted God's best for me and nothing less. God was faithful to every word I said. It's just His best wasn't what I was secretly hoping it would be.

God's best for you doesn't always align with your expectations or your ego. Sometimes you have to wrestle your ego and expectations to the ground and make them submit to the word of God. I've found the best way to do this is through prayer and gratitude.

I was raised with the admonition that every gift given to me warranted a thank you note. Well, God is the ultimate gift giver. James says every good and perfect gift comes from the Lord (James 1:17). God has never given me a gift I didn't come to appreciate in time. Thank God when He gives you a gift, even if you don't like it when you receive it. I guarantee you'll be thanking Him for it many times in the future.

You can pray for your ex to find "the One" if you have the heart to pray for it sincerely. But don't do it to prove you're "super saved and sanctified." If you do, when you start seeing your ex coupled up and happy on social media and/or in real life, it's going to burn.

Don't pray petty prayers. Pray powerful prayers that go beyond hurt feelings generated by your flesh. Pray for your heart to look like God's.

HOW DO I DO THIS?

Here are a few tips and techniques you can implement to begin praying more authentic prayers right now.

Set a standard for yourself that above all, you will approach the throne of God boldly. Don't be afraid to say to God "Here's what I have in my hands. Here's what I'm laying at Your feet. I want the rest you promised me. I'm unburdening myself to You and choosing not to unburden myself to people who knew 'us.' I'm not seeking validation for my decisions or opinions from man. I'm leaving this at Your feet. Work all things together for my good because I love You and am called according to Your purpose."

Ask the Lord to remove, restore, and renew. Is there something you need plucked out of your heart? **Ask God to remove it.** Tell Him if you're angry or bitter over your breakup or toward your ex. Let Him know you want Him to pluck this root of bitterness out of your heart. Tell Him if you can't pray for something because it would be hard or inconvenient to you. Ask Him to remove that seed of selfishness from your heart.

Has some essential part of your personality or a necessity for you to walk in faith been broken? **Ask God to restore it.** Share with Him your desire to be able to trust again, love again, or have an open heart again. God is a God of restoration. He specializes in doing exceedingly abundantly above what we can ask or think. He gives back more than was taken. Ask Him.

Have you become weary and worn down? **Ask God to renew you.** Making things new is another of God's specialties! When David is confronted about his sin with Bathsheba, he cries out to the Lord in repentance. He cries out for both restoration and renewal. He wants God to restore to him the joy of God's salvation and asks God to renew a right spirit within him (Ps. 51:10). We can do the same.

Write down what keeps coming up in your prayers. What is being revealed about the state of your heart? Are you still dealing with a broken ego, broken expectations, or hurt feelings? Are you still struggling with forgiveness? Have you fallen into a routine where you repeat the same phrases with no feeling or conviction? Pay attention to the patterns in your prayer life. This can highlight areas of weakness, stubbornness, or ignorance you need to address.

Acknowledge answered prayers. Many times, I've been so busy asking God to do something, I failed to acknowledge what He had already done. **When God answers a prayer for you, acknowledge it.** Thank Him for answering you. When I made it a point to acknowledge God and thank Him for what He'd done, I found more things to thank Him for. I began to search out and see His hand in everything. I became intentional about looking for Him to show up in the areas I begged Him to step into. My faith grew strong. I didn't question whether God would be there; I watched and waited for Him like I knew He was coming! The more we thank God, the more we realize we have more to thank Him for than we realized.

You get

what you

pray

for

Heart Break

(Rest)

Real, restorative rest doesn't look like hiding under covers or running off to the beach

Made to Lie Down

I SPRAINED MY RIGHT MIDDLE FINGER when I was in second grade. It was just before summer break, the night before field day. Field day was filled with outdoor activities like running with an egg on a spoon and hacky sack and three-legged races.

Michigan is one of those places where it gets hot in the daytime, but cools down significantly at night, especially in the early summer. We had old, wood framed windows that wouldn't stay up unless you propped them open. Since it was a school night, I had to go to bed while it was still light outside. Since it was still hot out, my mom left my bedroom window propped open with a thick branch.

Soon, I became engaged in a game of trying to get comfortable. With the window open, it was a little cool. I pushed the window up, removed the stick, and put the window down. But with the window down, my room was too warm. I pushed the window back up and wedged the branch in the corner. Back and forth I went.

Each time I ventured back to the window, my attention was snagged by the game of tag going on in the street below. All the kids whose moms weren't mean were still up playing in the fading light. I wanted to be outside playing, too. Each trip to open or close my window allowed me to live vicariously through the kids in the street.

I lifted the window up to see what everybody was getting to do that I wasn't a part of. I leaned against the windowsill, my fingers gripping the edge, tilting as close as I could get to the screen without touching it. I must not have put the stick in place correctly. The weight of the window knocked the stick out of the way. The sound of wood grating against wood was my only warning. I jerked my head back before the window slammed down, but I didn't move fast enough to save my hand.

I don't think I'd ever screamed that loud before that day, and I'm sure I haven't since. My stepdad ran up the stairs so fast he stumbled. He found me frantically trying to lift the window off my hand and pull my fingers loose. He freed me and examined the damage. My middle finger had taken the brunt of the impact and was already swelling. He left in search of ice.

"I told you to leave that window alone," my mother said as soon as she saw it. "If you'd taken your tail to sleep like you were supposed to, this wouldn't have happened." I found this sage pronouncement neither comforting nor helpful.

My mom had no sympathy in situations like this. She also had no intention of letting me stay home the next day.

"I don't think I should go to school. I'm really hurt."

"You're going to school."

"But Mom, it's field day. I can't—"

One Mama glare and a raised eyebrow later, I was standing at the school bus stop.

I went to school, but being my mother's child, and just as stubborn as she is, I made sure the teacher knew about my injury. She sent me to the principal, who called home. My mom sent my Uncle Morris to get me. They took me to the hospital. The x-ray showed my right middle finger, while not broken, was sprained. They put it in a splint. The splint was more painful than leaving it bare. It was uncomfortable to have my finger pulled straight in that way. It's because of that splint my finger is straight and fully functional, but that doesn't mean I appreciated it at the time.

I used to believe rest was the fun part. I pictured rest as lying on the beach with a fruity drink with an umbrella in it, snuggled down in my bed with a good book, or sinking into a bath after a long day. Self-care was getting a facial or a massage. Taking a break was a time out. It was running away from "real life" for a little while. But I've discovered that real, restorative rest doesn't look like hiding under the covers or running off to a beach for me.

When I broke up with my ex, I slept well for the first time in months. I started exercising more. Many of the thoughts plaguing my mind about our relationship evaporated. I felt physically and mentally refreshed. It felt like the break I needed. But I still felt a tiredness I couldn't explain. I realized the one thing I hadn't let rest was my soul.

I can't speak for anyone else, but my soul was worn out by the time I broke up with my ex. Too much time spent looking at what everyone else was doing and running hard to catch up had tired me out. Trying to outrun insecurities, fears, and negative voices depleted my stores of energy. I was exhausted from the exertion of trying to get my relationship to work because I'd invested my best into it and couldn't face losing it.

I thought ending the relationship would take the weight of all that off me and I could relax. I thought I would immediately feel rested and released.

Months after my breakup, after the initial lift of physical and mental rest, I came face to face with the hard truth that soul rest can't be bought or fought for; it's only found in Christ.

It wasn't until I began giving my burdens to Christ that I realized rest could be awkward and uncomfortable. It's only when you stop doing an exercise or carrying a load that you realize how tired you are. This is when you notice your legs feel like noodles and you can't catch your breath. Once you're aware of how badly you hurt, you may feel like you could never resume your workout. A similar process happens in breakups. You may be fine initially, but once you rest, pain you didn't notice before can make its presence known.

In my breakup season, many times I felt the urge to run, to get moving. When I rested, those feelings of pain were catching up to me. I could feel them gaining on me. I imagined I could feel them breathing on my neck. Insecurities I thought I had outgrown, fears I had pushed past to "do the thing," and negative voices of the past I thought I had conquered were chasing me down.

When you feel insecurities about how you look or who you are getting too close, long buried fears of never getting married or having a family getting out of the grave and stumbling toward you, or that thing Sister So-and-So said creeping up behind you, your first instinct may be to run to another relationship, get lost in lust, or become busy. Please don't.

If you've gone from relationship to relationship, you already know it doesn't alleviate anything. It's like you're looking for something you can't find. You're not asking for too much, but you can't seem to find this bare minimum love or consideration. It's not because all men are the same or all the good ones are taken. It's because what your soul really longs for is rest and restoration, and only God has that. You will never be filled or whole seeking anything but Him. You could find a man who ticks every box and it still won't be enough until you lie down, Sis.

In my personal bible study after my breakup, God kept me in Psalm 23 for a long time. One passage that stuck out to me was "He makes me lie down in green pastures. He leads me beside still waters. He restores my soul. (v. 2-3)."

For years, I rushed through these verses, seeing only the provision in the pasture. But in the season after my breakup, I began to see a fuller picture. Yes, there is provision you don't have to work for. You don't have to hunt, gather, till or toil for it.

But it says He makes me lie down in green pastures. I would go right past the pasture without God making me lie down. I wouldn't rest. I wouldn't relax. I wouldn't eat.

My natural inclination is to keep going no matter what. The tougher it gets, the harder I'm going to push to get it over with. But before big battles and long journeys, God calls His people to rest.

Maybe when God invites you to rest, you ignore Him in the same way. Maybe you're too busy looking at what everyone else is doing and "hustling" to listen to the Lord. "I have to hustle and make moves. Everyone else is already married. Everyone else already has kids. Everyone else has a home they love." You know Jesus calls you to rest but you already feel behind. You need to catch up. You push and press your way forward until something breaks.

In the next verse, David says "He restores my soul." Please don't think that by doing these three things, coming to certain realizations or learning to pluck and pull out negative thoughts or habits you will be able to restore yourself. You are not the restorer of your soul, Sis. That work is done by the Lord. The work of redemption belongs to Him alone. I don't want any woman reading this book to think she'll be completely healed and whole from every heartbreak she's ever suffered in relationships if she does everything exactly like I suggest. No new book, relationship, hairdo, or diet is going to do that. Only turning to the Lord will.

> 28 Come to me, all who labor and are heavy laden, and I will give you rest. 29 Take my yoke upon you, and learn from me, for I am gentle and lowly in heart, and you will find rest for your souls. 30 For my yoke is easy, and my burden is light." Matt 11:28-30

Jesus says He will give you rest. He says you will find rest for your soul. Wouldn't it feel fabulous to rest your soul? Not just your body or your mind, but your soul?

As someone who had body and mind rest without soul rest, I can tell you it's unfulfilling. It's a temporary fix at best and delaying the inevitable at worst. What you want is rest and restoration—body, mind and soul.

Maybe some of the breaks in your life and relationships came because you refused to rest like I did. Maybe you thought you were over your breakup a long time ago, but you still feel restless and weary. Perhaps you've been broken up for a while but you're still discovering new injuries and areas of brokenness. All these things spring from refusal to rest.

I used to think rest was a weekend getaway, getting lost in a good book, or a good night's sleep. I still enjoy those things and recognize the benefits of them. That's not the type of rest you'll find in the following pages. This is where you stop running and start facing things. This is where you give your burdens to Jesus and lie down in green pastures, yes, but it's also where you take Jesus' yoke upon you.

Getting Over It

How did you process, or "get over" the breakup?

A LOT of talking with friends, journaling, prayer, reading encouraging books, lots of self-care, and just allowing myself the space to grieve and feel everything I was feeling... I also wholeheartedly recommend counseling. I think being able to process with a professional is so helpful and healing.
💔 Katie H.

Lots of prayer and therapy. My mother and cousin and friends were very influential and helpful during this time. I prayed to the Lord to help me understand this loss and remember what I deserve. I knew from the start that He and I wanted different things. We had different values. I wanted marriage and commitment and he basically told me he couldn't give me that.
💔 Kacy S.

In all honesty the 2 things that got me through were reading the Bible daily and meeting someone else. There were times that I couldn't make it through the day without reading the Bible. It was my bread of life and my hope. And, not that I'm suggesting it, lol, it helped to meet another guy that I found myself interested in. It helped me realize that maybe there was someone out there who was a better fit for me, even if it wasn't that guy.

💔 Natalie M.L.

The only way I could get over it was constant prayer and counsel from my Bishop. I felt so lost spiritually, not understanding why God put me through this situation.

💔 Ayanna S.

Because I had so many deep-rooted issues at the time (looking back I can say that but at that time I couldn't see them), I think it made processing and moving on from the break up very difficult. I was a college freshman at the time and didn't have the outlook on life or the relationship with God that I do now.

Even though I had a relationship with Jesus at this point, it wasn't very strong, and I didn't realize how unhealthy my relationship was with this guy.

I think being separated from him during and after the breakup for several months actually made it harder to move on from him because of the anxiety and anticipation of when I would see him next and actually having the conversation about the breakup/getting the closure I needed. It honestly just took a lot of time and God working on my heart for me to get over the break up.

💔 Erica U.

That happened 4 years ago, and in many ways I'm still not over it! A divorce with a kid involved is so different because we still have to be involved in each other's lives, so old wounds seem to always stay fresh, and that's super frustrating.

But time helps, as cliché as that is. Lots of prayer, a strong support system of girlfriends, good examples of strong marriages to give me hope that I can have that again someday, and a beautiful little girl who reminds me that it all resulted in her coming into the world, so I can't regret ever being with him.

💔 Kelsey B.

I went through a period of depression. I was seeking solace in old friendships (that should have remained buried) and found out why they were no longer my intimate friends and needed to remain distant. I visited that "old man" so to speak. I thought I was getting over him, but I was only bringing misery and more pain to myself. Then I decided to try online dating, that was interesting.

💔 Cheryl S.

God helped me through all the way! It took a lot of leaning on Him, tears shedding, and reminding myself why I initially broke up with my ex in the first place. I had to find myself and learn to love myself. It was one of the best decisions I could ever make for myself. I found so much healing through my tears, prayer, the word of God and encouragement from others, like you.

💔 Andreana J.

A person

isn't a paycheck

you receive for

having principles

and being pure.

To the Girl Who Didn't Get What She Worked for

¹⁵ Then Laban said to Jacob, "Because you are my kinsman, should you therefore serve me for nothing? Tell me, what shall your wages be?" ¹⁶ Now Laban had two daughters. The name of the older was Leah, and the name of the younger was Rachel. ¹⁷ Leah's eyes were weak, but Rachel was beautiful in form and appearance. ¹⁸ Jacob loved Rachel. And he said, "I will serve you seven years for your younger daughter Rachel." Gen. 29:15-18

I'VE ALWAYS BEEN DRAWN TO SCRIPTURES about the life of Jacob, particularly scriptures pertaining to his relationships with Rachel and Leah. I admire how Jacob went to Laban and vowed to work seven years for Rachel. Can you imagine spending seven years of your life working for someone with only the promise of marrying their child as payment? The love Jacob felt for Rachel, the anticipation of spending the rest of their lives together, was great:

> So Jacob served seven years for Rachel, and they seemed to him but a few days because of the love he had for her. Gen. 29:20

Finally, the day Jacob had worked seven years for arrived. Jacob asked for what he'd worked for: Rachel (v. 21). Laban threw a big feast and gave his daughter to Jacob. Only there was a problem:

> 25 And in the morning, behold, it was Leah! And Jacob said to Laban, "What is this you have done to me? Did I not serve with you for Rachel? Why then have you deceived me?" Gen. 29:25

Jacob accused Laban of deception, and he was right to do so. Laban says in his country, they don't give the firstborn before the younger (v. 26). He knew this before he accepted Jacob's terms. Perhaps Laban believed Leah would find a husband in the seven years that passed. If this were the case, he could have mentioned this possibility to Jacob as it became clear their arrangement needed to change. So why didn't Laban mention their custom to Jacob?

It wasn't beneficial for Laban to tell Jacob! He knew Jacob didn't want to marry Leah, but his hard work over the years proved he was willing to work for Rachel. Laban gets an additional seven years of work and a husband for Leah out of his deception.

When you feel as if you've been deceived by the person you're in a relationship with, it changes your perception of the entire relationship. How long has this person been hiding their true self or motives from me? Has everything been a lie? Was this or that specific moment part of the deception? Deception can leave you frustrated and bitter, particularly when you've worked so hard for an outcome you now realize you were never going to receive.

There are several aspects of the story of Jacob and Laban that could be instructive for dealing with disappointment and deception. I want to deal with two of these in-depth here: Jacob's work and Laban's deception. I believe examining these two areas will provide a good framework for how to put the disappointment and frustration a woman may have after a breakup into perspective.

❤️ WORKING FOR THE REWARD

Jacob had been at Laban's for a month when the conversation about wages occurred. We can conclude from Laban's words that Jacob had made himself useful and served Laban in some way. Laban asks Jacob "what shall your wages be?" This allows Jacob to tell Laban how he wants to be compensated.

The terms were Jacob's. He decided that he would work seven years for Rachel. He worked diligently to fulfill the contract. To him, the years seemed like only a few days because he was motivated by his love for Rachel.

At first glance, this is a beautiful picture of a man willing to work for the woman he wants. It's what some women dream of, a man who's willing to pursue them single-mindedly. At second glance, it sinks in that Jacob is seeking to earn Rachel. She is his **wage.**

Everyone who works should be compensated fairly. If you enter into a contract and fulfill the terms, you should get what was promised for your service. Maybe you feel like that didn't happen in your last relationship. Perhaps you kept the terms of your contract, but your ex refused to fulfill his promises to you.

When I went through my breakup, I felt as if I had worked for years and was duped out of my wages. Instead of marriage and happily ever after, I was paid back in broken expectations and pain. It took me getting still and resting in God before I would admit two things that helped me to accept what had happened: 1) I hadn't gotten to the contract stage of the relationship with my ex; therefore, he didn't owe me any wages. 2) I wasn't trying to hold my ex accountable for what I felt I was cheated of. I was mad at God for not giving me the future I'd worked so hard for.

The bible speaks about wages in the New Testament:

> For the wages of sin is death...Rom. 6:23a

The devil does all he can to distract us from this fact. He lets us believe we will receive happiness, contentment, love, security, fame, or whatever else we desire if we work for sin. But when we go to collect our wages, all we will receive is death. Death is the only thing sin can pay us in.

God is different. A wage is something you earn. God doesn't owe us a wage. In fact, we owed God a debt we couldn't repay or work off. In His goodness, God sent Jesus to be the perfect sacrifice—the only acceptable sacrifice, so that we could be brought into the family of God.

The other half of the verse that says, "the wages of sin is death"?

> ...but the gift of God is eternal life in Christ Jesus our Lord.
> Rom. 6:23b

Everything God gives us is a gift, something which can't be earned. As God's children, He gives us gifts. While sin makes you **work** for the death and destruction you reap, God **gives** gifts, the greatest being eternal life in Christ Jesus.

The language of the bible illustrates that God gives freely:

> [7] "Ask, and it will be given to you; seek, and you will find; knock, and it will be opened to you. [8] For everyone who asks receives, and the one who seeks finds, and to the one who knocks it will be opened. [9] Or which one of you, if his son asks him for bread, will give him a stone? [10] Or if he asks for a fish, will give him a serpent? [11] If you then, who are evil, know how to give good gifts to your children, how much more will your Father who is in heaven give good things to those who ask him! Matt. 7:7-11

> Delight yourself in the LORD, and he will give you the desires of your heart. Ps. 37:4

> [16] Do not be deceived, my beloved brothers. [17] Every good gift and every perfect gift is from above, coming down

from the Father of lights, with whom there is no variation or shadow due to change. James 1:16-17

3 His divine power has granted to us all things that pertain to life and godliness, through the knowledge of him who called us to his own glory and excellence, 4 by which he has granted to us his precious and very great promises, so that through them you may become partakers of the divine nature, having escaped from the corruption that is in the world because of sinful desire. 2 Pet 1: 3-4

Do you know what I love about 2 Pet. 1:3-4? The fact Peter confirms God fulfills the great promises He makes. God has always clearly stated what He will do, and He fulfills His promises at the appropriate time. But at many stages of my life and my relationship, I chose to place my faith in someone who couldn't guarantee they would keep any promises they made to me. I didn't get payment up front; I just started working. I ended up being deceived because I wasn't discerning.

No one can guarantee they'll keep every promise they make to you. Humans are flawed. They often have good intentions and bad execution. I don't think my ex set out to deceive me. I also don't think my ex is the person who made me promises they couldn't guarantee they could keep. No, that was me.

I believed in my ability to "seal the deal." I worked hard in my relationship with my ex in the hope of maybe one day getting the role of his wife. I put all my best skills on display early and often: I cooked delicious meals, showed an interest in the things he enjoyed, and tried to make our relationship as convenient and conflict free as possible. I tried to look the way he wanted me to look. Every offhand comment was a clue to earning the promotion to wife.

I hope that doesn't sound familiar to you, but I have a feeling it might. Sometimes as singles we work so hard to be chosen. We hear and hold on to the hope and miss the message being clearly communicated. In my case, when the relationship ended, I realized all of that "work" wasn't even about the man I thought I wanted to marry.

> Losing my relationship hurt so bad because I lost **it**, the hope I wouldn't be single for the rest of my life, not because I lost **him**...because I couldn't put Mrs. before my name, not because I couldn't put his last name after.

I'm honest enough to admit at some point my focus switched from whether I should marry the man I was in a relationship with to the goal of getting married. I was going to make it to Mrs. if it killed both of us. I sinned in my relationship. I made an idol out of marriage. I lied. I stole from God, reallocating time, tithes, and talents I should have given to Him to sustain my relationship.

I went home tired at the end of each day from my exertions, but hopeful one day all my hard work would pay off. But all my hard work was rewarded with a broken relationship.

I had to learn a person isn't a paycheck you receive for having principles and being pure. I can't quote Matthew 7:7 about receiving what we ask for without being reminded of the truth of James 4:2-3:

> [2] You desire and do not have, so you murder. You covet and cannot obtain, so you fight and quarrel. You do not have, because you do not ask. [3] You ask and do not receive, because you ask wrongly, to spend it on your passions.

Would marrying my ex have benefited anyone but me? Would he even benefit?

I could have been a good housekeeper for him, but I didn't know how to be a good wife to him. I knew what all the books and social media memes said a husband needed from a wife, but I didn't know what **he** needed in **his** wife. When he was down, I couldn't lift his spirits. I couldn't respect him the way he needed me to respect him. I didn't appreciate him the way he needed me to appreciate him. I knew how to be **a** wife, but not **his** wife.

This is not to say he never failed to meet my expectations or that he knew how to be a husband to me. He did fail, and he didn't know. But maybe if I'd shifted my perspective and focused on whether I could be **his** wife instead of **a** wife, one or both of us might have figured out we weren't right for each other sooner.

If you worked hard for your ex and feel heartbroken it didn't end in happily ever after, know my heart is tender toward you. I understand how it feels to give something your all, only to fail. I know pain and anger might be speaking loudly right now, but I encourage you to tune in to the small voice inside whispering "maybe I'm so upset because I tried to make this happen in my own power. Maybe I tried to gain through work and works what I didn't trust God to give to me."

You need to ask yourself, "Did I, consciously or unconsciously, make a deal with God that I would get my ex in exchange for being a good Christian? Did I work so hard to love and treat everyone right because I thought the prize was getting to marry someone and have babies? At some point, did my ex stop being a person and become a prize or a worked for wage in my eyes? Was I so focused on the allure of a position that I missed the person?"

You must be brutally honest with yourself about your expectations and where they came from. When we don't get what we feel we worked for, it can prompt us to stop fulfilling the terms of the contract. You may begin to feel justified in engaging in unproductive or even sinful behaviors. These things become consolation prizes for not winning the ultimate prize. You might stop going to church, reading your bible, or praying. You might overspend or overeat. You might engage in attention seeking behaviors because you believe you deserve special recognition for being a Christian woman AND as single as a dollar bill. Other behaviors you may engage in: laziness, watching pornography, fornication, lateness, rudeness, or physical or verbal aggression.

Are you making doing the Lord's will look like a miserable life by your post breakup behavior? I understand your pain, but your issue isn't with the Lord. With all due respect, your issue is with yourself. God didn't promise you a man and a marriage for your obedience to Him when you decided to follow Jesus. You can't "hold God accountable" for what did or didn't happen in your relationship. You were in a relationship with a human being who had free will. Don't try to punish God when it doesn't work out. God doesn't owe you anything, yet He gives you everything. Maybe you should commit everything you are to Him—even your desire to be a wife one day.

💔 DECEPTIVE DEALS

There's a second aspect of the story of Laban's deception of Jacob I can't overlook. Laban deceived Jacob. No one would deny this. However, no one could deny that Jacob himself had been the deceiver several times in his dealings with other people, either.

Jacob was angry Laban deceived him, but Jacob tricked his brother Esau out of his birthright (Gen. 25:29-34). Jacob also tricked his father into bestowing Esau's blessing on him (Gen. 27:1-33). Jacob ran from Esau for years before they reconciled.

Maybe you feel as if you worked hard for a marriage you didn't get. Perhaps you're disappointed with the reality you woke up to. I get that. But also? Maybe you need to acknowledge that in some ways you have been a deceiver. I know that sounds harsh. You might be thinking "I would never do to anyone what my ex did to me." I'm not here to insist you've lied to, cheated on, abused, stolen from, or broken someone. But I am here to get you to examine yourself honestly.

One of the ways you might have been deceptive is to pretend to be things you weren't. Have you ever pretended you had skills or experience you didn't have to land a position you technically weren't qualified for? Have you pretended to have likes or desires a potential spouse had? Have you pretended an interest in a sport or hobby you didn't like to bond with someone? You might have done these things because you really believed you were the best person for the position, but your motivation or intention doesn't make your actions any less deceptive.

You might fool people with your deception, but you won't fool God. When I was busy unto the Lord instead of working onto Him, hoping to be blessed with what I wanted, He knew my motivation. He knew my reasons for wanting to be married had nothing to do with illustrating the relationship between Christ and His church to the world.

He knows when you want to get married to post pictures on social media and be #relationshipgoals. He knows when you're depending on a person for security and provision and not Him. He knows when you've made an idol out of an institution He established with purpose for His glory.

This is not to say deception doesn't work. This doesn't mean every marriage you see was entered for the right reasons. Yes, there are women who worked hard for a husband and received one. There will always be exceptions to the rule, and the devil does give the illusion of getting what you work for. But we must remember who we are supposed to be and who we serve. We must remember everything we receive from God is a gift, even if that gift means saying "goodbye" to something we worked hard to obtain.

Where is the Lie?

EACH BREAKUP IS AN OPPORTUNITY to reexamine ourselves, to come to a new understanding of who we are, right now, in this moment. That's one of the good things about breaking up. How are you going to change how you see and present yourself before you're back in a relationship again?

Many of our problems in relationships stem from lies we accepted as truth based on the relationships we observed or encountered in childhood or experienced throughout our lives. These lies aren't limited to what we learned from our relationships with our parents or our past relationships; we must consider all the relationships we've witnessed or experienced in our lives. We must consider moments between strangers we witnessed that stuck with us as well as what someone tried to instill in us through their words. All these things are significant.

What did you learn about relationships when you were younger? What did you see growing up? How might this be affecting your performance in or success with your current relationships? What lies have you believed about yourself that threaten to cripple you in your romantic relationships?

THE LIES THEY TELL

♥ YOU'RE TOO MUCH/NOT ENOUGH

People will volunteer many reasons why relationships won't or don't work. They will posit all kinds of theories about why you're single. Many of them are meant to be complimentary, but when we start to believe these things, they can be detrimental.

For example, one thing people told me all the time was I was "too smart". Men didn't like women who were as smart as I was. Family members used to make fun of my crush on one individual. They would say if I married him, I would come home from work with news I cured cancer, and he would proudly tell me he learned to tie his shoes that day. I was too smart for him.

In middle school, I got into a debate with a friend. "You like all these guys who are never going to like you," she yelled at me. "You aren't cute enough to attract the guys you want."

The seeds of these two thoughts—that I was too much and not enough—took root.

Perhaps you've internalized notions that you are too much, not enough, or both. The ways you're too much and not enough will vary from what others experience, but maybe some of these oft-repeated ones will resonate with you:

- You're too intimidating.
- You're not assertive enough.
- You're too independent.
- You aren't independent enough.
- You have too much debt.
- You don't make enough.
- You have too much money.
- You're too career-driven.

- You don't care enough about career advancement
- You're not attractive enough.
- You're too attractive.
- You're not smart enough.
- You're too smart.
- You don't care enough about your appearance.
- You're too concerned with your appearance.
- You talk too much.
- You don't communicate enough.

Internalizing these lies about ourselves can lead us to believe the bigger lie that we aren't balanced enough for real, true relationship. Once we perfect ourselves, the right man will fall from the sky and the angels will sing about how Heaven sent him especially for us. This isn't just detrimental because it keeps us chasing a perfection we'll never achieve; it's an outright lie.

There have been and always will be women much less together than you who have successful marriages and happy families. There have been and always will be women much more together than you who don't have a successful marriage or happy family. I want to be the best version of myself I can be when I get married, but I don't believe God is waiting for me to get it together before He blesses me with a husband. God used men who were hot messes, completely unqualified for the tasks God gave them. Don't believe the lie God needs you to be perfect to reflect the relationship between Christ and His bride, the Church.

❤ YOU HAVE TO SETTLE

Another lie people attempt to perpetuate among single Christian women is that our standards are too high. I remember watching a dating show with a picky woman where a friend of hers was trying to get her to lower her standards a bit. "Jesus is taken," she said. She went on to list several men who would be considered a great catch who were also taken. Her message was clear: you're not going to get perfection. You're not going to get the best. You're going to have to settle.

When I was younger, people told me men my age weren't ready for the type of relationship I desired. I needed to wait patiently for them to reach my level of maturity. I suppose the purpose was to put the onus on men or make them the problem, but sometimes this has the opposite effect.

When people say, "Men aren't ready for that type of commitment," instead of responding "I'll wait for someone who is," many women consider lowering their standards to meet men where they are. They are convinced they want too much and no one will measure up to what's usually a simple and attainable list of attributes. They morph into mathematicians, developing theorems full of "if, then" statements written to suit specific conditions. Maybe if a man has this but not that, they can still accept him.

When you go into a relationship with the intent of settling, you will usually end up disappointed. You are starting the relationship slightly dissatisfied with your partner because they don't meet all your requirements. It becomes their fault that they aren't all you want them to be. You end up trying to build a relationship based on "taking an 'L.'" You're even more upset when the relationship doesn't work out because you didn't want the person in the first place. More than likely, someone else will benefit from all the mental and emotional capital you poured into building and growing this person into what you wanted.

You can become angry, bitter, and disillusioned when you settle for less because of the lies people tell you. Maybe you comprised on your core values and threw yourself out of alignment with who you knew yourself to be, only for the relationship to fail. Don't take your bitterness into another relationship; call out the lie that says you have to settle for less or be alone forever.

Much of the violation I felt after my breakup was a result of the compromising I made for the relationship. When you do things you don't want to do or that go against who you are to have a relationship, when that relationship breaks up, all you are left with is guilt, shame, and remorse. You wish you had stuck with what you knew to be true. When you know better, you wish you had done better.

THE LIES WE TELL

Having deficient or incorrect instruction in relationships can lead us to lie to ourselves. Not only do we have to contend with what others have impressed upon us, we must also deal with the assumptions and conclusions our subconscious accepts based on this flawed information. Here are a few of the relationship lies I told myself for years. Maybe some of them will sound familiar to you.

💔 LOOK FOR COMPLETION, NOT COMPLEMENT

For many years, I looked for someone to complete me instead of for someone to complement me. I wanted to find a mate who had the characteristics I lacked instead of one who would complement or enhance what I already had. Because I believed the lie I was not enough in some areas and too much in others, I also believed I needed a mate who would make up for my areas of weakness.

I let limiting beliefs about myself box me in. For example, instead of believing I was naturally gifted in English but could also learn to excel in other areas, I believed the lie I couldn't excel in STEM subjects (Science, Technology, Engineering, and Math). I was reluctant to attempt anything involving technology. My ex worked in the field of information technology, and I leaned heavily on him for anything remotely technical. I jokingly referred to him as Tech Support.

I had found an individual who would compensate for my areas of weakness instead of finding someone who would push me to become the person I was supposed to be. Since I've been single, I've learned how to use technology to accomplish tasks I thought were far beyond my reach. Once I stopped believing the lie, I was able to pursue growth in this area.

The interesting part of the lie I told myself about my lack of technological skill is that before I met my ex, I worked as a technical assistant and was the go-to girl for all things computer related at the company. Yet I convinced myself I wasn't skilled enough in technology and I needed a man to take these tasks over for me.

💔 ASPIRATIONAL DATING

Based on past relationships and experiences, you might learn to chase people who are what you believe you should be. When you look for someone who is what you think you should be, you look for someone who is successful in ways you aren't. Though it seems you're chasing a person, you're really chasing after a better version of yourself. You find out if you want to **be** a person instead of if you want to be married to, and aligned **with**, a person. This is not a healthy way to seek a relationship.

For me, it was the opposite. I didn't want to date someone who was like the person I thought I should be. I went after someone who would want the person I wanted to become. Unfortunately, instead of motivating me to become the best version of myself, this merely brought up issues I thought I had successfully conquered.

Breakups demonstrate that the things you think you've defeated still have you under their control. Worse, they can confirm the awful beliefs you thought you'd overcome are still present and fully functional.

When I thought about my last relationship, one thought kept asserting itself: He fit what I felt about myself. He didn't fit what I wanted to feel about myself, but what I actually felt. I told myself I was over people telling me if I tweaked this or that about myself, I would be marriage material. I was past pronouncements of "You'll never get married because... (fill in the blank). I was self-confident, or at least I was trying to be. Somewhere there was someone who wouldn't want to change everything that made me "me."

Those old issues began to creep into my relationship not long after it began. I was smart and funny, but there was one thing that made him hesitant to take the next step in our relationship. What he wanted wasn't outrageous, but it was familiar. Eerily so. It echoed the criticisms of the past like voices in an empty high school hallway.

How I viewed myself was warped long before I met him. My thoughts about my marriageability were inculcated in grade school. I had worked hard on my self-esteem and finding my value in Christ. I thought I was comfortable with who I was. But my ex became a mirror that reflected how I really felt about myself. The things he said matched the thoughts in my head. I wanted him to fit what I wanted to believe about myself, and instead, he fit what I felt.

After my breakup, I realized I could continue to be mad at him for not loving the person I was enough to accept me, love me, and want to marry me, or I could tell myself the truth. I had expected his love to inspire me to improve myself for him. This wasn't realistic, nor was it fair.

How dare I demand someone love me more than I was willing to love myself? How dare I expect him to choose me and treat me better than I treated myself? I wanted his love to be the catalyst for me loving myself. I was hustling backwards with no idea why I wasn't moving forward.

I chose a man who would want the woman I aspired to be instead of the woman I was. I shouldn't have been surprised he didn't choose me when I wasn't who he wanted. The reason I was almost his perfect woman was because I was almost the perfect version of myself. But when it comes to committing yourself to someone for as long as you both shall live, almost isn't enough.

Maybe you've been in this position, wanting someone who wants the woman you could be if you would just do a, b, or c. Maybe you expected him to treat you how you should feel you deserve to be treated. Perhaps you were smacked in the face by the reality your ex didn't treat you any worse than how you treated yourself. Perhaps he treated you exactly like you believed you should be treated. Maybe, like me, you chose a man who would marry the woman you're striving to be in a heartbeat but would never be sold on you in your current state. If you, too, were hustling backwards, it's time you to a step forward.

Be honest with yourself. Now's not the time to run to another relationship to make you feel whole for all of five seconds. It's time to deal with who you are. It's time to do what you may have thought you'd already done: get healed and whole by the power of Christ.

Your ex was a mirror for you. Maybe the mirror was broken. Maybe the mirror was simply reflecting your brokenness back to you. Maybe both of you were, are, broken. I don't know what's true for you. But whatever kind of mirror he was, he is no longer the mirror you see yourself reflected in.

Now, you should be peering into the word of God and the character of Christ to inspect your reflection. The word of God is not cracked or broken; what you see reflected is exactly what's in front of it. God's word will show you your true self. No matter what you see, know God is ready and willing to forgive, to cleanse, and to draw near.

You see, when you're baptized into Christ and have put on Christ according to the scriptures, you're justified and sanctified by the blood Christ shed for you. God sees Christ's sacrifice when He looks at a Christian. He sees the Holy Spirit dwelling in you. Christ mediates on your behalf, and the Spirit prays to God for you with groanings that can't be uttered.

♥ VALIDATION IS FOR MORE THAN PARKING

Another thing a woman can be taught is to seek approval or validation from relationships, either from her mate or for her choice of a mate.

It was important to me that other people thought my ex was a great match for me. I was proud when people noticed how well-suited we were to one another. It proved I knew what I wanted and validated my decision-making abilities.

Although other's opinions of my relationship was important, my ex's validation was more important. I needed someone to choose me, to pick me. Being my ex's girlfriend proved I was someone worth pursuing seriously. Many women end up in subpar or even abusive relationships of all kinds based off the fact someone said something to them they desperately needed to hear. They will date a man they wouldn't normally consider simply because he chose them. This bleeds over from familial relationships, friendships, and previous relationships.

People who seek validation in relationships are seeking things another person can never provide them with — security, happiness, joy. They make a person responsible for providing their entertainment and enjoyment of life in quantities no one could meet.

You would be surprised how adept people can be at zeroing in on this weakness and exploiting it to their advantage in relationships. They see your need for constant validation, or your dependence on their "skills." They know you will always need their "help" to accomplish certain tasks. They will realize they can manipulate you by withholding what you think you need if you don't do what they want. In contrast, a man who is whole and looking for a marital relationship will either avoid you altogether or leave you before the relationship progresses too far. He will see your symptoms and take steps to protect himself from your sickness. And yes, selfishness, needing to be entertained, flattered, or validated, insecurity, dependency, and low self-esteem are sicknesses.

Selfishness not only kills relationships, it misplaces our focus. This self-attention isn't forcing us to compare ourselves to Christ or to be more like God created us to be; it's encouraging us to compare ourselves to other flawed humans.

TRUTH BE TOLD...

One thing I've learned about myself since my break up is I employ temporary fixes to fatally flawed logic because it's easier to change the paint color than to break up the foundation and start over again.

"I don't know who I am anymore." This thought ran in my head at the end of 2016 into early 2017. I'd been in Orlando nearly ten years, in a relationship nearly nine years, and at the same job for nearly eight years; all of a sudden, none of those long-term identifiers applied to me. Things which shaped what I did and how I saw myself were stripped away in a matter of a few hard months. I was looking in the mirror and asking myself "who is Erica Denise Hearns, 32, single, no kids? What is she called to do? Who is she called to be? What does she like? Where is she going?" I asked the questions, but I didn't have any answers.

Instead of dealing with the weighty questions this realization brought up, I retreated. When you experience an identity crisis, there are a few quick fixes to employ, and I employed them. My aunt gifted me an appointment with a natural hairstylist for my birthday. I was so used to straightening my hair because that's how my ex liked it that I didn't know what other styles might look good on me. Finding out how I'd like to wear my hair took on monumental importance. It became paramount to my identity. "I don't know who I am" went from a deep philosophical exploration I should sit in for a while to a series of "would you rather" questions of preference.

The deep work of discovering who I am transformed into something much more share-worthy on social media. I could Instagram my new hairdo, the new recipe I tried, or the new place I visited. I couldn't find as good of an image to go with my avoidance of thinking about where I belong and what I should do with my life.

I found myself policing what I liked on social media. Others could see what I liked. What would my liking this say about me? Would someone think I was too sad, happy, or bitter? Will I get text messages or DMs or phone calls asking me to take something too raw and honest down?

The #unfiltered life where you're always moving on to bigger and better things is hard to keep up with when you haven't moved on to bigger and better things. I haven't moved on to a new relationship; instead I'm sitting with myself, trying to understand what my last relationship taught me about who I really am and what I really need in a partner. I'm doing the deep work, and most days it looks like treading water and looking in all directions to figure out which way lies the closest shore.

If you find yourself in a similar situation, don't be afraid to be honest with yourself about that. You don't need to possess every answer, but you should at least be asking the right questions. More importantly, you should be honest about the answers you have received. Find the lie and uproot it. You'll keep repeating this painful cycle until you do.

To the Girl Who Was Betrayed

BETRAYAL IS RAMPANT IN THE BIBLE. Brothers betray brothers, stealing birthrights and blessings without conscience. Brothers sell the brother they loathe and lead their father to believe he's dead. Sisters battle each other for the attentions and affections of the same men. A mother loses her child and lies in an attempt to take another woman's child. David orchestrates the death of Uriah in a bid to cover up his sin. Jesus is betrayed by one of the twelve who walked closest to Him. Another of the twelve denied knowing Jesus three times while Jesus was being beaten, mocked, and crucified.

People betray one another in ways great and small all the time. But when betrayal ends an intimate relationship, the wound feels a little deeper. This is someone you thought you knew, someone you trusted. This is someone you shared with, prayed with, and thought would be in your life forever.

Betrayal is marked by a loss of trust. This loss of trust always hurts, but it's even more painful when paired with a loss of confidence in your ability to discern who is trustworthy. The strongest person can feel weak and small when they learn their trust has been violated.

When people in the world find out their significant other betrayed their trust, they might seek retribution for the wrong done against them. Those who want retribution search for ways to inflict the pain they feel on anyone they believe is involved in the betrayal. Whether they depend on "karma," "the universe," or take it upon themselves to visit this pain on the betrayer, they expect the betrayer to suffer. They rest in or react to the notion the people who hurt them will "get theirs."

Whether the "crime" is lying, cheating, infidelity, swindling money, or being a thief of their time, some women are prone to seek vengeance and vindication. This retaliation may include destruction of personal property, malicious posts on social media and websites, physical assault, child custody disputes, and other legal matters.

But as Christians, we are a peculiar people. Our actions should line up with what the Word says, not what the world does. Years ago, there was a movement in popular culture where everyone was asking themselves "What would Jesus do?" Anyone curious about what Jesus would do should be able to look at how Christians respond to situations for their answer. Yes, we're all human and fall short, but we should be striving to exemplify Christ.

Some Christians don't "fall short" in this area—they run full tilt toward sin. They can't wait to "cut up," "go off," or "act a fool." They "wish somebody would" betray them. They're saved, but...They are representatives of Christ, disciples called to teach, baptize, and teach again, but they let their flesh dictate their actions when they feel disrespected. No one is going to treat them any way they want to and think it's cool.

If this describes how you react to betrayal, I have to ask: have you read God's word?

Joseph was betrayed several times. He was betrayed by his own brothers. Their jealousy of him caused them to put him in a pit and plot to kill him. One brother spoke up and stopped his death, but Joseph was then sold into slavery.

During his enslavement, Joseph was lied on, lied to, falsely imprisoned, and forgotten. Potiphar's wife lied on Joseph and had him falsely imprisoned. The other prisoners whose dreams he interpreted were supposed to remember him, but they forgot about him.

Even so, what God showed Him and told Him came to pass. Even so, when he was in the position of power and his brothers had to come to him for help, he helped them. He embraced them. He gave one of the greatest statements on divine providence and purpose recorded in scripture:

> As for you, you meant evil against me, but God meant it for good, to bring it about that many people should be kept alive, as they are today. Gen. 50:20

Joseph saw how God worked everything together even when people plotted against him.

Can you see that? Can you see past your hurt and ask yourself what good God means to bring out of your situation? You may know and quote "all things work together for good to them that love God, to them who are the called according to His purpose (Rom. 8:28 KJV)," but do you believe it? Has the truth of this statement sank into your soul yet? You say you love the Lord and you're called, but are you ready for "all things?"

"All things" means bad things will happen, things that will hurt you or strip you of your ability to trust if you allow them the opportunity. The promise isn't "bad things won't happen." The promise is those bad things will work together with the good things, and the net result will be good for you. Everything in your life has a purpose, but sometimes we need to shift our perspective to see it.

In the Sermon on the Mount, Jesus teaches the people foundational truths and principles for living. He starts with what they already know. They know what the law says. Even so, Jesus phrases each statement "you have heard it said" or "it has been said." This is usually followed with the phrase "by them of old time." People had gotten away from the law. It had become something that "them of old time" would say.

There were people in the crowd who knew the law to the letter, yet Jesus deliberately phrased it this way, I believe, to show that while some knew the **wording** of the law, they didn't understand the **spirit** of the law or the **purpose** for which the law was given. For example, the scribes and Pharisees, who claimed they knew the law, are shown their lack of understanding and even hypocrisy by Jesus several times in scripture.

Each time Jesus quotes the law in the Sermon on the Mount, He adds the phrase, "but I say unto you." He's letting the people know there's more to following Him than following the letter of the law. Not committing murder isn't enough; Jesus deals with the thoughts and intents of the heart and the character of the person. Many people who aren't Christians don't kill people because it's against the law, but few understand the call not to be angry at someone without cause. Jesus wasn't concerned with the **appearance** of godliness but the **heart**. He called His disciples to be different.

When Christians break up because of betrayal, even though it may hurt them the same as it would anyone else, they walk it out—live it out—differently. People are watching to see if you're going to live up or down to their expectations of a Christian. If you do the same things the unsaved do, you ruin your witness to those observing you. We have to approach this thing from another angle. We must ask what Jesus would do...and **do** that.

What would Jesus do if He was betrayed? If only there was a story in the bible of Jesus being betrayed that we could examine to determine how we should respond when someone betrays us. Of course, we do have such a story. Jesus was betrayed many times in scripture. Jesus was betrayed by a member of His inner circle, one of the men who walked closely with Him (Matt. 26:45-50). All the disciples forsook Him and fled when He was arrested (Matt. 26:56). Peter denied Jesus three times, the last so strongly he cursed (Matt. 26:69-75). Jesus entered Jerusalem to shouts of praise days before He was met with cries of "Crucify Him!" None of this was news to Jesus. He knew it was coming. But that doesn't mean it didn't hurt.

The biblical example Jesus exemplifies is consistent. He knew one of His disciples would betray Him and told them so (Matt 26:21). Yet he didn't banish Judas from His circle. He knew certain things had to happen in order for the scriptures to be fulfilled. He knew Peter would deny Him three times before the cock crowed and told Peter so (Matt. 26:33-35; Lk. 22:33-34). But Jesus also let Peter know He had prayed for him (Lk. 22:31-32). When Peter cut off the ear of one of the men who came to take Jesus, Jesus healed the man's ear and let Himself be taken away (John 18:10; Lk 22:50-51). Even as He hung on the cross, Jesus said "Father, forgive them for they know not what they do (Lk. 23:34a)."

Jesus didn't have a problem with discernment. He knew what was in people's hearts. But even with this knowledge, Jesus forgave offenses and treated the individual as if the offense hadn't or wouldn't happen. He prayed for His enemies. One of His last acts on earth was to pray for the people who were killing Him. Yet many of us can't forgive a person lying to us, "cheating" on us in a dating relationship, committing adultery in a marriage, or deceiving us.

Jesus modeled going beyond the **appearance** of holiness and being a follower to **being** holy and a disciple. Some of us are so busy "following" Jesus, all we're doing is following: walking around observing what Jesus is doing without any impact on our lives and situations. We're following to see a miracle or obtain a blessing. We aren't being disciples, students of the Lord who are apprenticing under Him. We haven't dedicated our lives to living out the principles He teaches. We haven't given ourselves to teaching others and persuading them to accept Jesus' invitation and be obedient to Him.

We look holy. We keep God's commands on the outside. We draw near with our lips but are hearts are far from Him (Matt. 15:7-8). We say we are saved and set apart, but when it comes time to do the hard, holy things like forgive, leave vengeance with God, pray for those who hurt us or despitefully use us, repay evil with good, bless those who curse us, and deal with our hearts so evil doesn't leave our lips about someone, we want God to know our heart. We want the spiritual equivalent of a participation trophy. Worse, many of us want to be on the roster of the championship team and receive a ring without ever taking off our warmups and getting in the game.

Christianity will cost you something, and you need to count the cost and check your bank balance before you decide to buy in. You put your ability to tell someone off in the pot to pay for this Christian life. Your life is no longer your own. You were freed from sin to become a slave of righteousness (Rom. 6:17-18). Whatever you do, you are serving someone. The time has come to choose whether you're going to serve your faith or your feelings, the eternal God or your ego.

Those of us who serve Jesus deal with betrayal the way Jesus teaches His followers to deal with it. No matter how mad we get or how much it hurts, we do the hard thing and forgive. Not for them.

Not even, as some would say, for ourselves. We forgive because we were forgiven. We forgive because the same measure with which we forgive, we will be forgiven. We don't allow betrayal to make us bitter because we know the purpose being wrought in our lives is bigger than any person or incident. We see the bigger picture. Our view is different, so we act differently than those in the world.

God is gracious to His people even when they're bitter against Him.

Dear Bitter Betty

I NEVER SAW IT BEFORE I HIT IT.

Most people look for deer or wild hogs on the roads here at night. Those types of hazards are expected. No one expects to encounter literal crap on the road.

One night while moving personal items from Orlando to my new city, I drove through crap. I have no idea how it got on the road. What I can tell you is on one of the last stretches of road before my destination, I found myself driving through crap. It sounded like driving on wet pavement after a summer rainstorm. I could feel the muck slowing my tires. The smell came through my air vents.

When I got out at my destination, the stench was overwhelming. Manure coated my car's tires, wheel wells, and chassis. Days passed before the smell went away.

Everyone who got within a few yards of my car was in no doubt I'd driven through something. I related the late-night experience to my aunt as we approached the scene of the incident the next morning. When we rode past the stretch of road, it was clean. The same area coated with crap hours before looked almost pristine. There was no evidence to corroborate what I said had happened at all.

Sometimes a breakup can be like my experience that night. Everyone who gets close to us gets a good whiff of a bad fragrance, but when we try to show them the manure we've come through, there's nothing there. All that's left of the experience is a stench we can't seem to get rid of.

It took me a long time to realize bitterness was the cause of this odor. Like most women, I flinch away from the label of "bitter." I don't claim it; I deny it. I lift my hands in a defensive gesture and back away slowly from such a pronouncement. I reframe my words and actions, defend and justify myself. Call me anything but bitter.

But I was bitter. I wasn't witty, sarcastic, caustic, "real", honest, or a hard truth-teller. I was bitter.

Let's look at some of the definitions of bitter:

1. having a sharp, pungent taste or smell; not sweet:
2. (of people or their feelings or behavior) angry, hurt, or resentful because of one's bad experiences or a sense of unjust treatment:
3. (often used for emphasis) painful or unpleasant to accept or contemplate:

In an article for Psychology Today entitled "Don't Let Your Anger 'Mature' Into Bitterness,"[2] clinical psychologist Dr. Leon Seltzer explains the origin and evolution of bitterness. He posits bitterness begins as hurt. When you believe the cause of your pain had a malicious intent, you can experience anger and resentment. Left to fester, anger and resentment become bitterness.

Are you bitter? Are you trying to mete out the justice and

---

[2] Selter, Leon F. "Don't Let Your Anger 'Mature' Into Bitterness" Accessed March 16, 2018 (11:00am), https://www.psychologytoday.com/blog/evolution-the-self/201501/don-t-let-your-anger-mature-bitterness

vengeance that belong to God? Are you too busy pursuing justice to do what God told you to do? You aren't praying for this person like God told you to because you don't want them to have any blessings. You don't want them to repent and give their lives to Jesus because you don't want to have to possibly walk past them in heaven.

You claim you have been restored and made whole, but are you letting your need to be bitter bar you from having a home in Heaven? Are you saying, "I would love to forgive everybody, treat everybody right, live in peace among all men and do everything I can to be with Jesus, but only if my ex gets what he deserves because he hurt me on purpose"? With all due respect, sis, who cares? Is he worth missing Heaven?

You can't grab on to or apprehend the reason God called you if you're still holding on to hurt and bitterness with both hands. But it can be difficult to let go of what someone has done to you. So how do you do it?

Bitterness shows up in the bible in several different passages. It is often described as a root, as in the passages below. I have included a couple counter verses to demonstrate the kind of roots Christians should have:

> [10] The heart knows its own bitterness, and no stranger shares its joy. Prov. 14:10

> [12] Therefore lift your drooping hands and strengthen your weak knees, [13] and make straight paths for your feet, so that what is lame may not be put out of joint but rather be healed. [14] Strive for peace with everyone, and for the holiness without which no one will see the Lord. [15] **See to it that no one fails to obtain the grace of God; that no "root of bitterness" springs up and causes trouble, and by it many become defiled;** [16] that no one is sexually

immoral or unholy like Esau, who sold his birthright for a single meal. [17] For you know that afterward, when he desired to inherit the blessing, he was rejected, for he found no chance to repent, though he sought it with tears. Heb. 12:12-17 (Emphasis added)

[16] If the dough offered as firstfruits is holy, so is the whole lump, and **if the root is holy, so are the branches.** Rom. 11:16 (Emphasis added)

[16] that according to the riches of his glory he may grant you to be strengthened with power through his Spirit in your inner being, [17] so that Christ may dwell in your hearts through faith—that you, **being rooted and grounded in love,** [18] may have strength to comprehend with all the saints what is the breadth and length and height and depth, [19] and to know the love of Christ that surpasses knowledge, that you may be filled with all the fullness of God. Eph. 3:16-19 (Emphasis added)

[25] Therefore, having put away falsehood, let each one of you speak the truth with his neighbor, for we are members one of another. [26] Be angry and do not sin; do not let the sun go down on your anger, [27] and give no opportunity to the devil. [28] Let the thief no longer steal, but rather let him labor, doing honest work with his own hands, so that he may have something to share with anyone in need. [29] Let no corrupting talk come out of your mouths, but only such as is good for building up, as fits the occasion, that it may give grace to those who hear. [30] And do not grieve the Holy Spirit of God, by whom you were sealed for the day of redemption. [31] **Let all bitterness and wrath and anger and clamor and slander**

be put away from you, along with all malice. [32] Be kind to one another, tenderhearted, forgiving one another, as God in Christ forgave you. Eph. 4:25-32 (Emphasis added)

The above examples are found in sections where a person's conduct is being discussed. These admonitions are meant to equip the hearer with knowledge that will assist him in living a holy life. In every instance, the root of bitterness must not be allowed to grow; instead, we are to be rooted in love, tenderhearted and kind toward one another, and to strive for peace. Bitter roots can't bear sweet fruit. To be holy, you must have holy roots. It's time to banish Bitter Betty, sister.

Here are three appearances of bitterness in the bible which address how bitterness might show up in your life, and what to do to turn your inner Bitter Betty into a Sweet Sarah.

WHEN BITTER IS A PERSON, PLACE & TOTALLY A THING

❤ PERSON

One word the bible uses that translates to bitter is Mara. Mara is the name of a person and a place in the bible.

Mara is the name taken by the mother-in-law of a biblical heroine. When this woman returns to the land she'd left years earlier, she renames herself Mara. Mara is better known as Naomi, the mother-in-law of Ruth. When Naomi and Ruth arrive in Bethlehem-Judah, the people see them and ask, "is that Naomi?" Naomi's response is telling:

> [20] She said to them, "Do not call me Naomi; call me Mara, for the Almighty has dealt very bitterly with me. Ruth 1:20

Naomi wants to be known as Mara, or bitter. She doesn't acknowledge she left God's people and land to live among a heathen nation because she didn't trust God to provide. She operated outside of God, yet when tragedy befell her, she blamed Him.

A lot of women become bitter like Mara when their relationships end, forcing them to return to a place they thought they'd left for good. They don't want anyone to see them and say "hey girl, is that you? What are you doing back here?" They don't want anyone to say, "What happened to that guy you were dating?" "What did you do to run this one off?" "I knew that relationship wasn't going to work." They don't want to hear the curious and hurtful "You're STILL single?"

Whether they say it or not, everything about their attitude and countenance says "I don't want to be here. I'm not happy here. I'm only here because the Lord has dealt bitterly with me."

Many women feel like God has dealt bitterly with them when their relationships don't work out. They judge whose "side" God is on based on the successes and failures experienced by themselves and their exes after the breakup. They determine who was at fault or "wrong" by scrutinizing their ex via face to face interaction or social media. Whoever appears to be doing well after the breakup is obviously the one God stands by and supports.

This scrutinizing and ascribing feelings to God is not helpful, and it definitely isn't biblical. Hardship is not always an indicator of sin or God's absence in a person's life. It is not synonymous with punishment. People experience hardship due to the consequences of sins they have repented of and been forgiven for. They experience it when God is growing their faith or developing them in some way. It's difficult enough to see what God is doing in our own lives; we don't need to analyze what He might be doing in anyone else's.

If your ex's life suddenly seems to be all "achievements unlocked", new levels attained, "glow ups" and other positive achievements, it can be difficult to keep your anger from maturing into bitterness. This can be an especially difficult battle if your relationship was plagued by lying, cheating, verbal/emotional abuse, or physical abuse. Seeing the person who inflicted so much pain on you experiencing success in life can make you bitter if you aren't careful to pluck out the root of bitterness before it gets a chance to grow.

If your ex's life appears to take a turn for the worse after your breakup, you may feel as if he's getting what he deserved. In this scenario, some women seek to elevate the importance of their former position in the ex's life. They begin to believe they were "the blessing" in their ex's life. Again, hardship does not always equal punishment. Even if their hardship is punishment, you have no idea what they are being punished for. God is the one who blesses and curses. He makes His rain fall on the just and unjust. Vengeance belongs to Him. It's none of your business.

Additionally, doing better financially or materially doesn't always mean you are blessed. Appearing to do better via social media doesn't mean you **are** doing better. Many women are growing bitter over things that only exist on social media and have no connection to reality.

Whether their newfound wealth exists or not, God is the One who determines who does better or worse by both spiritual and worldly standards. God is the one who sees what is done in a person's private life and rewards it openly. We will all have to give an account for the deeds we have done in this life. We won't be held responsible for what anyone else did. It does no good to keep an account of all your ex did to hurt you. It won't be a sufficient excuse for why you didn't do what God called you to do. It can't justify your sins to the Lord. All holding on to hurt can do is make you bitter.

God can place people in our path to reflect truths about ourselves back to us. If we don't cultivate the ground of our hearts to be receptive, this revelation will cause us to grow hard, dry, and bitter.

The same drought conditions that drove Naomi to leave God drove her back to where His people were. Naomi didn't trust God to provide for her in a time of drought, so she chased provision. Though this move seemed to satisfy her needs initially, depending on what she could see eventually failed her. She expected God to go with her where He never sent her, and she was so angry when He didn't she blamed the tragedy that befell her on God.

The physical drought in the land is similar to the spiritual drought of those who operate in their own strength while expecting God to bless the mess they make of their lives.

Some people let their heart get so dry and bitter they can't accept the love, respect, and consideration the person God would send would give to them. Instead of seeking out the water of the Word and getting used to absorbing love, they chase mirages in the desert. They go around saying "I'm thirsty. I'm thirsty." Yet when someone offers them living water, they're afraid to drink it.

Through Ruth's obedience, Naomi was eventually blessed and able to drop the label of "bitter." God used Ruth, whose presence in Naomi's life only occurred through Naomi's running away from hardship, in His plan to bring Jesus into the world. God is gracious to His people even when they are bitter against Him. He truly works all things together for the good of those who love Him and are called according to His purpose.

💔 PLACE

The children of Israel came out of Egypt and encountered Marah. After they crossed the Red Sea on dry land, they traveled three days in the wilderness with no water. When they finally came to a place with water, they discovered the water was bitter. They couldn't drink it. They named the place Marah. God showed Moses a tree to cast into the water. The tree made the bitter waters sweet (Ex. 15:22-27).

This scenario is similar to what many women experience in relationships. They think they've finally found what they're craving and looking for, but once they taste it, they realize it's bitter.

Maybe you thought you'd found "the one" ... but you were wrong. Maybe you thought threatening to break up with your ex would force him to see he needed you...but he didn't. Few things hurt worse than thinking you've found what you've been searching for, only to realize that while it looks the same, it doesn't work, taste, or feel the same.

The children of Israel who encounter Marah feel so much disappointment, they murmur against Moses. Maybe you're doing that. Maybe you're murmuring against what led you out of your relationship, wondering what's next.

Moses cried out to the Lord about this bitter water. God shows Moses a tree to put into the water that makes the water sweet. Once we add God into the mix, He can make what is bitter sweet. You don't have to stay bitter. You don't have to remain dry and thirsty. You don't have to be upset about leaving a relationship that wasn't in God's plans for your life, or question why God called you to walk away from it. God still has a life for you. It's usually waiting on you to get in line and obey what He's told you to do.

When we come to a place of bitterness, we must cry out to the Lord and let Him show us how to make it sweet.

❤️ THING: HEARTS

Experiences will harden your heart, like the Pharaoh's experiences with Moses. Every encounter hardened Pharaoh's heart against letting the people go. The more he saw signs and wonders, the more he dug his feet in. He couldn't go back on his word because of what it would mean. Letting the people go to praise God would be admitting their God was as great as or greater than the gods of Egypt.

Who was their God that Pharaoh had to let the people off work to serve Him? How could Pharaoh go back to his people and tell them to worship him as a god when he has bowed to the demands of the Israelites and their God?

Refusing to let go can make you bitter. Maybe you've placed idols above the sovereign God. Perhaps you are so busy catering to and serving them, you can't heed the voice of the Lord. Many women's lives proclaim they worship material gain, having a husband, and keeping up with the Joneses instead of the One true God.

Maybe you feel as if you can't go back and admit you need God. You can't let your attachments go because you're afraid they're all you have. Like Pharaoh, you attempt to pit your puny idols against Almighty God. You seek out those who seem capable of duplicating what God has done instead of admitting you were wrong.

This way lies destruction. Don't let your heart become hardened. Don't let your conscience be seared with a hot iron (1 Tim. 4:2). It can be too late. God can turn you over to a debased, depraved mind

(Rom. 1:28). The day you hear His word, harden not your heart (Heb. 3:15).

Many end up with bitter, hardened hearts because they won't heed the voice of the Lord. They keep telling God they can do it themselves, and when they fail, they reap a bitterness of their own making. It doesn't have to be this way. Don't be hearers only. Do what the Word says, and you won't have to taste the bitterness of the destruction wrought by a hardened heart.

I will *bring* my *whole* self, not my *hole* self to my *relationships.*

#repeat

Breakaway
(Run)

I want to *count the cost* and *judge expediency,* not *refuse to try* because *I'm afraid.*

Set in Slippery Places

NOT EVERY BREAK YOU EXPERIENCE WILL BE BONE DEEP. Some of them are in areas without bone, but they're not any less painful or broken. I experienced such a "break" when I was in middle school. My cousins were down from Lansing visiting for the summer and we decided to play at Shirley & Willard Park down the street from my house.

This jungle gym had a big, twisting slide, monkey bars, a swing set and a steel double slide. The sides of the steel slide were melted together in the middle, creating a thick seam.

My cousins and I were too big to use the slides the way they were intended. We ran up and down both sides of the slide, gliding down on our tennis shoes. Every now and then one of us would slide off and end up with our backside in the dirt, but we kept on playing.

I was chasing one of my cousins around the jungle gym when it happened. My cousin ran up one slide; I ran up the other. I was more than halfway up the slide when I reached for him and missed. The extension upset my balance and my foot slid out from under me. I didn't have time to catch myself before momentum and gravity drove my face into the place where the slides met.

I slid all the way to the bottom. Blood gushed like a geyser from the middle of my bottom lip. It swelled up like Eddie Murphy's in the movie **The Nutty Professor**. It was quite embarrassing. It didn't help that I bawled like a baby.

Two of my cousins grabbed me by the arms and walked me home. When we were less than a block away, I heard one of my relatives exclaim "Oh, Lord!" As the accident prone one, no one was surprised I was hurt and crying.

My mother was militantly against taking me to the doctor, and I can't say I blame her. It seemed I was always going to the ER for some weird injury. And here I was with another one. Mom, with the wisdom of mothers who know cuts in the mouth heal faster than anywhere else on the body, decided it wasn't worth the hospital bill and slapped a Band-Aid on the middle of my swollen lip. She told me to put some ice on it. Despite my outraged cries, this was all the first aid my injury received.

You would think I would learn something useful from this experience like don't run up a slippery slide. Just go up the stairs next time, even when you're playing tag. Or better yet, don't play tag. But what I gleaned from this experience was that if you have to stretch for something, don't bother. You're just going to end up getting hurt.

This wasn't the first time I'd gotten hurt stretching for something. I stretched for that boy on the bed and broke my arm. Here I am now with a busted lip for reaching just a little bit outside of what I was comfortable with. I should stick with what's in easy reach.

This led to years of only going after what I knew I could get. I stuck with what I knew I was good at. I never willingly got uncomfortable. I bored myself to death.

That is the exact antithesis of what I want for myself, and for you. There's so much more abundance and purpose in life outside of where we're comfortable. We can't let mental limitations keep us from stretching, from reaching further. The saying is true; the things we want **are** outside of our comfort zone. We have to be willing to reach and go hard for what we want. That's what separates those who find from those who don't.

I love this verse about finding God: If you seek me you shall find me if you seek me with your whole heart (Jer. 29:13). Maybe after a breakup, you find yourself doing things halfheartedly or being overly cautious. You were comfortable with the ripping. You didn't like it. You found yourself in the midst of a breakup, so you worked through it. You were comfortable resting in God, communing with Him and allowing Him to restore you. But now when I'm talking about reaching and running, breaking out of the box and getting out of your comfort zone, your instinct is to shrink back. You don't want to date another guy who a, b, or c. You don't want to try again. If you had to dip seven times like Naaman, you've dipped six with no results. You're struggling to believe dipping a seventh time will be any different.

That wasn't the first time I had tried to run up that slide. I had run up the slide before. I could tell you that from that moment on, every time I saw that slide, I thought about busting my lip. I could tell you I thought about the pain and how I never wanted to feel it again. I could tell you I never ran up that slide again.

I could say all those things, but I'd be lying. I ran up that slide again chasing someone else. I didn't think twice about it. With the resiliency of a kid, I tried again. The more times I tried it and didn't fall or slide down on my face, the less that memory surfaced.

That isn't to say I don't remember it; I remember it vividly. Even now, I imagine I still feel that knot under the center of my lip. But even though I can recall it perfectly and it was something that changed my life in ways I couldn't have known at the time, I moved on. I've done things a hundred times more dangerous since then.

We have to keep going. Maybe I won't run up a slide again, but I will pursue other ways to cut time and catch the illusive thing.

Making a break is trying. It's being open. Some of the breaks in my life have compromised my freedom. Indeed, there are considerations other than the fact I am free to do things. Paul says we are free to do what we want but not everything is expedient (1 Cor. 6:12; 10:23). Everything isn't going to profit me. I won't gain anything or find an advantage in everything. But if I choose not to do something, I want it to be my choice. I want to count the cost and judge expediency, not refuse to try because I'm afraid.

I could continue to bore myself. I could continue to go to work, church, and home. I can choose not to be open to men outside of what I've had before. I can choose not to be open to men who resemble men I've dated before. I can decide to live in the same track and not do anything different...or I can make a break for it. I can be open to new experiences and trying new things. I can be open to meeting new people who may not look, act, or think like I do, who may have something of value to share with me or show me.

The whole point of making a break for it is to get out of the norm and try something new. To feel the fear and do it anyway. Be open to love and dating again. Try something new. Let a friend set you up.

Go on a blind date. Meet someone online. Attend a meetup or join a club. There's no shortage of places to go and things to do if you're not afraid to meet people.

I don't have a problem meeting new people; I wrestle with the fear I'm meeting the same people in different skin. I'm afraid the same thing that happened in my last relationship will happen in a new relationship. But if this season has taught me anything, it's to stop being so afraid and to trust the work God has done in me.

This section isn't just about finding a new love. It's about truly breaking away from the mistakes of the past and looking at the future with fresh, hopeful eyes. Your past is already broken, so try something new. Find a new career if you want one. Move to a new city if that is where God is leading. You have been set free. And there is no reason you can't try something else or go somewhere else. Respond to the nudges you are getting. Make a break for it.

If this season has taught me anything, it's to stop being so afraid and to trust the work God has done in me.

Lesson Learned

What's the most important thing you've learned from a break up?

One lesson I've been learning is that God doesn't waste anything...and so I've been hopeful to believe He will redeem and restore the ashes from the break-up I experienced...for my good and His glory.

♥ Katie H.

The most important thing I learned from a break up is that time heals all and better is coming. It may not be right away, but you loved once, and you will love again. Our best days are ahead of us and just when we think we will never find someone as good as the last, someone walks into our life that changes everything. I am clinging to God and clinging to hope during my single season of waiting.

♥ Kacy S.

I think what I learned most from that particular break up is that I should have listened to God sooner. I think it was a harder break because we were together longer. I remember a specific instance about a year before where I felt like He was asking me to give up that relationship and I didn't obey. I realized that no matter how much I tried to make it work, it wasn't what was best. And now that I'm married to Josh I'm so happy God didn't allow me to stay in that relationship any longer!!!

♥ Natalie M.L.

The most important thing I learned is that everything has a purpose! Figure out the lesson and you'll find peace!

♥ Ayanna S.

The most important thing I've learned from a breakup is how important it is to guard your heart; emotionally, spiritually, physically. You don't know until engagement or in some cases your wedding day if the person you are with is the person you are going to marry. Anything can happen, and that's why it's so important for God to have the first place in your heart.

♥ Erica U.

First, don't plan your life too far in advance. I thought I knew what the rest of my life would look like, and it all changed in the blink of an eye. Literally one day I was seemingly-happily married trying to start a family, and the next day I was pregnant and single staring motherhood in the face – alone.

Second, a strong support system of friends + family is SO important. Without their help, encouragement, prayer, and

shoulders to cry on, I wouldn't have made it. The friendships formed + strengthened in that season mean more to me than most.
♥ Kelsey B.

To not worry about what others say, focus on how they make you feel.
♥ Cheryl S.

What's meant to be, will be. If it's not, then know that your greater is coming. They were just mere carbon copies of the real deal to come.
♥ Andreana J.

let us also *lay aside*

every *weight*, and *sin*

which *clings so*

closely...

Hebrews 12:1

Forgiveness: Not for the Faint of Heart

HAD I KNOWN ALL OF THE "FOLLOW UP FORGIVENESS" I would have to extend, would I have forgiven? I asked myself this question when I discovered yet another abuse of my trust committed by someone close to me. The betrayal was months old, but the knowledge of it was fresh, and so was the pain. I had already forgiven so much, and here I was being asked to cover another debt. If I had known it would involve all of this, would I have forgiven that first trespass as readily? Would I have opened up my heart to this person again so quickly? And if I chose to do it again, would that mean I was to blame for the pain I experienced each time they took advantage of me?

When you first break up with someone, it's difficult to imagine life months or years down the road. If you do, your version probably doesn't include still dealing with issues brought up by the breakup. It likely doesn't involve repeating the forgiveness cycle again and again, from discovery to processing to forgiving. It may be impossible to imagine a time you can treat your ex as if they'd never offended you or trespassed on the private property of your heart.

What no one told me when I broke up with my ex was that unlike financial debts, the sum of emotional debt or grievances is rarely known when forgiveness is extended. While a bank or credit card company knows exactly what's owed before they extend forgiveness of the debt, those who practice forgiveness in a spiritual and emotional sense are often clueless about the extent of the debt they are forgiving. It could be months, even years, before they discover some of these debts.

You need to be aware forgiveness isn't a one-time deal. Follow up forgiveness is often necessary. There's not a limit on it. When asked how many times one should forgive, Jesus said seventy times seven (Matt 18:22). When you're hit with multiples of the numbers for completion, perfection, and completeness of order by Jesus in response to a question, things get real. Seventy times seven may equal four hundred ninety, but what Jesus is really getting at is forgiveness is continual.

This isn't the only time Jesus gives His disciples and the crowds following Him instruction regarding forgiveness. As mentioned in "Prayer: Not for the Petty of Heart," Jesus taught that we will be forgiven in the same measure as we forgive others. If we don't forgive, God will not forgive us. I can't speak for you, but I don't want to be on the receiving end of condemnation and judgment from God because I refuse to forgive an ex who violated a non-covenant relationship. I don't want to be subject to the wrath of God because a guy hurt my feelings and isn't sorry about it.

The times I've struggled the most with forgiving someone have occurred when I felt they weren't sorry for what they did. It's one thing to accept an apology and try to move on; it's another when no apology is offered. There's something about an individual turning your world upside down and then going about his or her life as if nothing special happened that can create a slow burn of bitterness and lack of forgiveness in a heart.

I saw a quote on Instagram about how men are promising their new woman the same world they still owe their old significant others. Most women won't care about the **promises**; they heard the same lines. It's the **execution** that bothers them. When a hurting woman sees her ex doing things for the new girl she was pressing him to do for her, it can feel like seeing someone who owes you money spending lavishly.

Often, people are willing to forgive debts they think a person can't pay, but when they realize the person could pay them but decided otherwise, they might get angry. Someone owes you an emotional debt you're supposed to forgive, yet they're spending lavishly on someone else? Seeing this might make you question if they didn't offer an apology because they don't believe the offense is worth addressing.

Anytime you invest a significant amount of financial capital into a venture and it becomes successful, you expect to be paid dividends on your investment. However, many women witness their investment of emotional capital maturing and paying out to the next woman. They no longer have access to the time, energy, effort, and money they poured into their ex, and they haven't been compensated for the gains their investment produced. They may have little to no emotional capital to invest in a new venture. They are being asked to forgive debt when they themselves are in emotional bankruptcy. Yet the command from Christ is still the same.

I could be super Christian and state the bible says to forgive quickly, but forgiveness is complex and needs to be fully understood if you and I are ever going to practice it. You need to know forgiveness isn't conditional, once for all time, or only when you have enough to spare. It's not for the weak or the stubborn.

You may be asked to forgive what you once categorized as unforgiveable. The discovery of each previously unknown violation of trust or willful disregarding of your feelings will start the cycle anew. Even if you've already sought the Lord in prayer, seen the counselor, and worked your way toward forgiveness, you'll have to do it again. It's painful and not fair.

One of the realizations I came to when processing the "fairness" of forgiveness was many of us have no idea what we're doing when we forgive. When I say something isn't fair, a little voice whispers "fair to whom?" Do I really want things to be fair and balanced?

I thought I did until I realized what that would mean. You see, fairness would be someone getting what they deserved. If you do something wrong, then you have to pay the price and suffer the consequences. I don't really want that. I want forgiveness.

If God meted out to me what I deserved, there would be weeping and gnashing of teeth for eternity. But because of the sacrifice of Christ, I can be justified, sanctified and forgiven. It wasn't fair that He who knew no sin became sin so that I could have a hope of salvation (1 Cor. 5:21). It wasn't fair at all. But I thank God He saw fit to accept the substitution of Jesus, the perfect sacrifice, in my stead.

If I sin now, I can confess my sin and God will forgive me. The same way I want God to forgive me, I need to forgive. Even if I have to grit my teeth now, it's infinitely better than gnashing them later.

There was a woman I heard speak about abstinence and celibacy at a spring retreat when I was in college. She was a newlywed, married for a year or two, with a new baby. She spoke about the usual things for such a session. She and her husband had waited until their wedding night and it was the best decision they could have made. This alone would serve as a beautiful example of what God can do with a surrendered life, but in the ladies' breakout session, she shared something I've never forgotten.

I saw the full glory of God and how He had worked in this woman's life when she shared her past. She and her husband had waited until their wedding night, but her wedding night wasn't the first time she'd had sex. She was sexually active before she came to Christ. It's not uncommon to hear such stories, especially now. But what stood out to me was how honest she was about her continued struggle with guilt and sorrow. She sobbed on her wedding night because of what she could never give to her husband. He would never be her first. God had done great things in her life and with her story. God had forgiven her, but she was still struggling to accept that forgiveness. It was this struggle that made her so passionate about speaking to young women and urging them to value their purity.

This is another layer of forgiveness we might wrestle with: guilt. Many women are weighed down by decisions they made years ago. They've repented and confessed. God has forgiven them and cleansed them of all unrighteousness. But they can't let the guilt go. It's as if they believe if they release the guilt they won't remember what they've been delivered from and will repeat the cycle.

Guilt is a virulent disease and hard to get rid of. It can also be indicative of a lack of faith. If you truly believe God's word, that if you confess and repent, He will forgive, what more are you waiting for or expecting before you "forgive yourself"? Is your judgment more righteous or holier than God's? Are your standards higher than His? Who's the real lienholder on your debt, and who really has the power to forgive it?

Sometimes women believe they are over a transgression or shortcoming until the offense or pattern shows up again. They may react out of proportion to the current manifestation, then feel confusion. "Why did I snap at him/her like that? Why am I crying over this? Why am I so hurt over this? I got over this a long time ago, so why am I feeling this way?" They may say they are "healed, sanctified, and fortified by the Holy Spirit," etc., but when confronted by the same situation they've already overcome, they realize they are still "coming over."

How do you keep forgiving, releasing, and letting go when things keep cropping up? Does the continued reoccurrence mean you didn't truly forgive the offense the first time?

I'm going to be real with you: you may need to repent because you've been harboring offenses in your heart. Maybe you didn't forgive them the first time. You were supposed to leave the offenses at Jesus' feet in prayer. However, when you got up from prayer, you picked them back up and put them back on. You wonder why you don't feel relieved of a burden you refuse to put down. Those of you who wear offense like your favorite coat, who have been refusing to cancel the debt someone owes you, need to repent and accept God's forgiveness. You also need to forgive and let the offender go.

However, the need to forgive again isn't the same as the need to forgive the first time. Having to forgive the same person for a different offense doesn't mean you didn't truly forgive them the first time. It means you need to forgive them for this thing, this time. As new issues come up, you must forgive and release them. It means a lot of prayer on your part and the part of others. It means getting into the bible and seeing what God says about the issue. It might mean fasting. It might require professional assistance from a Christian counselor or licensed mental health counselor. Ultimately, it means acknowledging and being aware of that ultra-Christian notion we may not want to acknowledge: that God has forgiven us of so much.

Paul says of himself and others like him "Christ's love compels us (2 Cor. 5:14 NIV)." The fact God commended, or demonstrated, His love toward us in that while we were still sinners, Christ died for us (Rom. 5:8)? We are responding to that love. Jesus says, "If you love me, keep my commandments (John 14:15)." The things we've done to God are bigger and far worse than what has been done to us, yet God has forgiven us. As his children, He expects us to extend forgiveness for the relatively minor transgressions against us, not because of the person who offends us, but because of His extension of forgiveness to us.

People often say, "I'll forgive, but I won't forget!" That sounds good, but there's a tiny problem. The nature of forgiveness is simple: when you forgive someone, you treat them as if the offense has never occurred. God separates our sins from us as far as the east is from the west. As far as the east is from the west means two points traveling in opposite directions that never meet. You can't keep the offense connected to them. We pray that God forgives and forgets our trespasses and makes us new, but we want to keep someone else tied to their old man.

Forgiving and forgetting doesn't mean someone won't be judged. Indeed, the bible states clearly judgment is coming. But it also tells us why judgment hasn't come yet:

> The Lord is not slow to fulfill his promise as some count slowness, but is patient toward you, not wishing that any should perish, but that all should reach repentance. 2 Pet. 3:9

God's holding the door open, not because He isn't going to do what He said He would do, but to give everyone ample opportunity to be in the ark of safety before He does it. Being forgiving is not being a doormat; it's trying to extend to others what's been given to you, a chance or opportunity to be better. It gives them a chance to come to you fresh, without your judgments, and be something else.

I love this about Christianity. We have been transformed by the renewing of our mind (Rom. 12:2). We were once practitioners of a host of sinful things that kept us from inheriting the kingdom of God, but we have been washed (1 Cor. 6:9-11). If we're in Christ, we've become a new creation (2 Cor. 5:17). We get to be better than we were before. What we extend to people when we forgive is the same opportunity—the opportunity to be someone better.

Sometimes people associate forgiveness and forgetting with a lack of discernment. This isn't God's intent. The Word of God is described as a discerner (Hebrew 4:12), and the Christian is called upon to discern. Don't be misled: all things are naked before the Lord (Heb. 4:13). When God asks you to forgive someone, He knows all the things you don't know you'll have to forgive in the future. When Jesus says forgive seventy times seven, He knows all the foolishness you will encounter. God is not unaware of the cost of what He's asking us to do, but He has a purpose for our forgiveness.

Ultimately, yeah, forgiveness is for you. It's for your good. It's to make your load lighter. It's to release hurt, anger, and bitterness so your hands are free to accept the love, peace, and joy God wants to give you. It's all the clichés. But above all, forgiveness has been and always will be an act of love—not for the person who wronged you, but for the Person who saved you. It's not love for yourself but love and gratitude for all God has done and will do. This love compels you to forgive. We forgive to show others the love of Christ so they, too, might see it and desire to be saved.

PRACTICING PRACTICAL FORGIVENESS

Practical forgiveness can be summed up in one thought: not exacting punishment for wrongs or offenses. It's not holding someone up to be condemned for their actions. Forgiveness is when you could humiliate someone or make them pay what they owe...and you don't. It's what we see happen when Jesus encounters the woman caught in adultery: having the opportunity to condemn and choosing to save. Yes, this woman committed a sin deserving of condemnation, but when she is brought before Jesus, His response is to offer her the opportunity to "go and sin no more." Jesus didn't come to condemn, but to save (Jo. 3:17). Maybe if we had this mindset, if we were mindful of this mission, someone could see Jesus in us.

Stop seeking to condemn. Instead, look for ways to extend forgiveness. Allow someone to save face or their reputation, livelihood, or lifestyle. Your obedience to the call to forgive quickly and continuously could save someone's life, both physically and spiritually.

In Acts 16, Paul's steadfastness saves the life of a jailer both physically and spiritually. When an earthquake opens the doors of the prison and unfastens their bonds, Paul and Silas stay put. The jailer draws his sword to kill himself because he thinks they escaped, but Paul calls out and lets the jailer know the prisoners are still there. Paul didn't take the opportunity to leave a tough situation, and because of that, a man's life was saved. This man and his household then believed in Christ and were baptized because Paul refused to run.

Running from the command to forgive could cost someone the opportunity of eternal life in glory with God. That someone could be you. God is clear: if you don't forgive, he won't forgive you. I can't speak for you, but for me, God's forgiveness is worth much more to me than appeasing a broken heart. Don't run from what's required because of what transpired. Forgive, forget, and repent.

My *worth* was *determined* by the *price Jesus paid* for me on *Calvary.*

Emotional Net Worth

IN THE FINANCIAL REALM, people understand the need to diversify their portfolio, eliminate debt, build up their savings, and plan for the future. This knowledge doesn't always translate to how they operate in the emotional and spiritual spheres of their lives. People hesitate to think of relationships as transactional. They don't tend to think of emotions or feelings in terms of currency to be invested, saved, or expended to pay down debt.

Calculating one's emotional net worth before investing and expending their emotional capital in a new relationship is a crucial step many women skip in the healing process. Just as you shouldn't make a big financial investment without checking your credit and determining your budget, you shouldn't sign up for a relationship without ensuring you have the emotional capital to meet the expense.

Not all aspects of relationships will fit neatly into this framework, but it's an angle worth examining. How many times have we been in a relationship—with a friend, family member, or romantic partner—where we've found ourselves short of emotional funds to deposit into the relationship? I can't speak for you, but I know I've been emotionally overextended, or "upside down," because of the relationships I chose to invest in. These expenditures drained me and made me feel I had nothing of value left to give another relationship.

Unless you've done the work to achieve a positive emotional net worth, you're not ready for a new relationship. You can't afford one. You will have experience after experience of having your card declined for insufficient funds. Worse, people who have direct access to pull from your emotional account automatically—kids and dependents—will keep your account in overdraft status and incurring fees.

How do you calculate your emotional net worth? What factors do you need to evaluate to determine if this quotient is positive or negative? How do you improve your emotional net worth? How do you decide what to spend, invest or save? How do you eliminate emotional debt? These questions provide the framework to this section.

♥ HOW DO YOU CALCULATE EMOTIONAL NET WORTH?

Like financial net worth, emotional net worth is calculated using several categories. The ones we will explore in-depth are emotional debt vs. credit, investment, and profits. Net worth is determined by adding your credits together (savings, investments, assets, and liquid currency), then subtracting your debts. A positive net worth occurs when what you have is more than what you owe. A negative net worth occurs when you owe more than you have.

Emotional net worth, like financial net worth, can be improved two ways: decrease your debt and increase your assets. A popular method of achieving a positive net worth instructs participants to pay down debt and build up savings in tandem. I have used this method as a loose model to frame the discussion on eliminating emotional debt and building up emotional savings.

♥ LEARNING TO COUNT

> [27] Whoever does not bear his own cross and come after me cannot be my disciple. [28] For which of you, desiring to build a tower, does not first sit down and count the cost, whether he has enough to complete it? [29] Otherwise, when he has laid a foundation and is not able to finish, all who see it begin to mock him, [30] saying, 'This man began to build and was not able to finish.' [31] Or what king, going out to encounter another king in war, will not sit down first and deliberate whether he is able with ten thousand to meet him who comes against him with twenty thousand? [32] And if not, while the other is yet a great way off, he sends a delegation and asks for terms of peace. [33] So therefore, any one of you who does not renounce all that he has cannot be my disciple. Lk. 14:27-33

Following Christ, being a disciple of His, comes at a cost—a cost clearly spelled out in scripture. Jesus urges those who wish to follow Him to sit down and count the cost before agreeing to be His disciple. Don't find yourself unable to finish what you start and be mocked for you inability to finish. Don't go into a battle you can't win.

The exhortation to count the cost assumes you know how to count. You know how to count carnally, but do you know how to calculate your net worth biblically? What is considered a profit and what is considered an expense in God's economy?

The apostle Paul gave his perspective on the topics of loss and gain in Philippians 3:

> [3] For we are the circumcision, who worship by the Spirit of God and glory in Christ Jesus and put no confidence in the flesh— [4] though I myself have reason for confidence in the flesh also. If anyone else thinks he has reason for confidence in the flesh, I have more: [5] circumcised on the eighth day, of the people of Israel, of the tribe of Benjamin, a Hebrew of Hebrews; as to the law, a Pharisee;

> 6 as to zeal, a persecutor of the church; as to righteousness under the law, blameless. 7 But whatever gain I had, I counted as loss for the sake of Christ. 8 Indeed, I count everything as loss because of the surpassing worth of knowing Christ Jesus my Lord. For his sake I have suffered the loss of all things and count them as rubbish, in order that I may gain Christ Phil. 3:3-8

The entire conversation around profit and loss is flipped on its head when you examine verses like the above. Paul counted every positive attribute he had according to the flesh as a loss and rubbish. The worth of knowing Christ, obtaining Him, is worth the loss of everything else.

If you lost your relationship and gained Christ, amen. Knowing Christ is worth more than your social standing, career, or relationships. Christ asserts anyone who doesn't hate their family and even their own life can't be a disciple of His (Luke 14:26). God will have no other gods before Him (Ex. 20:3), including idols of your own making.

Christians endure the hard things for the profits they yield. The price of the process is nothing compared to the growth and gains of your net worth when you remain steadfast in your faith. You can count every trial you fall into as joy because you know the testing of your faith produces something valuable—patience. When patience has its full effect, you will be spiritually mature, complete, and entire, lacking nothing (James 1:2-4).

What you don't count as a Christian is the wrong done to you. Remember, love keeps no record of wrongs (1 Cor. 13:5 NIV). The word translated as "thinketh" in the King James Version and "keeps [no] record" in the New International Version means to reckon or count. To reckon means to put something to someone's account, whether in their favor or something they must answer for. Christians don't reckon with people; they leave that to God.

If you're keeping track of what others "owe" you in the hopes of increasing your net worth when they pay you back, it's time to put the calculator down, sis. Get rid of the spreadsheet of slights. Choose to concentrate on calculating your net worth based on what God sees as profit and loss.

EMOTIONAL PROFIT

The definitions of words translated as profit, profitable, or profited in the bible are advantage, benefit, usefulness, serviceable, and advantageous. When the Bible speaks of profit, particularly in the New Testament, it's referring to a gain that is an advantage or benefit. In other words, what you receive is somehow better than what you gave.

The dictionary definitions of profit as both a noun and a verb are financial. One definition is the amount you earn minus what you spent to manufacture, produce, or buy the product or service. Another is the money earned from an investment.

♥ ADVANTAGE/BENEFIT

Many of the verses using the word "profit" express the idea that there are advantages or benefits to making specific choices.

> 36 For what shall it profit a man, if he shall gain the whole world, and lose his own soul? 37 Or what shall a man give in exchange for his soul? Mk. 8:36-37 KJV

Your most valuable asset is your soul. There's nothing of comparable value. Gaining the world would not be advantageous if the price is your soul. This exchange will always result in a net loss. Don't end up with a negative net worth by trading the most valuable thing you have for less than it's worth.

> [63] It is the spirit that quickeneth; the flesh profiteth nothing: the words that I speak unto you, they are spirit, and they are life. Jn. 6:63 KJV

The flesh doesn't give you an advantage or benefit. It's not useful. There is no gain in the flesh. Living carnally, listening to your flesh, doesn't benefit you in any way. It only leads to destruction, pain, dissatisfaction, and weeping and gnashing of teeth. But the words of Jesus, the Word of God, are spirit and life. They are living and active (Heb. 4:12) and they give life. They are the ultimate advantage.

♥ THE ADVANTAGE OF BEING BROKEN

When Jesus instituted the Lord's Supper, He told His disciples the bread represented His body which was broken for them (1 Cor. 11:24 KJV).

The purpose of breaking bread is to have pieces to share. Sometimes we are broken to be shared. Perhaps break ups break us into pieces so those pieces can feed people. Maybe seeing our brokenness illustrates and illuminates the fact Jesus' broken body and the blood He shed for us weren't losses, but instead are the greatest advantages man has ever been given.

When we are in fellowship with Christ's suffering and crucifixion, when we crucify our flesh daily, we are in a prime position to give ourselves away in the service of the Lord. If the breaks you've experienced give you a common starting point from which you can help another person journey closer to Jesus, can you truly consider that a loss?

The principle that joy is birthed from or obtained through endurance is exhibited several times in scripture. A person endures trials, tribulations, and tests of faith and strives to remain faithful in the fires of affliction because they know what they obtain on the other side is drenched in joy.

Your pain produced spiritual profits! What you've been through is capital the person you've become can contribute to the cause of Christ. Don't despise having been broken; use it to your advantage.

♥ EXPEDIENCE

In First Corinthians, the Hebrew term translated as profit in the previous examples is translated as expedient, helpful, or beneficial in passages addressing the liberties, or freedoms, of the Christian. Expedient means likely to give you the result you want in a given circumstance. This definition refines one's understanding of a profitable course of action. It's not only advantageous; it gives you the results you want.

> [12] All things are lawful unto me, but all things are not expedient: all things are lawful for me, but I will not be brought under the power of any. 1 Cor. 6:12 KJV

> [23] All things are lawful for me, but all things are not expedient: all things are lawful for me, but all things edify not. 1 Cor. 10:23 KJV

Everything is permissible but not everything is going to gain you what you want.

1 Corinthians 6 addresses the physical body. The body is a temple of the Holy Spirit. The things you do, the sins you commit, are outside of the body, except the sin of fornication, which is committed with the body. Your body is a part of the body of Christ. Sexual intercourse is joining your body with the body of another. Will you join the body of Christ to a prostitute? When you fornicate, you join the body of Christ to a person of ill repute through an illicit act.

In 1 Corinthians 10, Paul is addressing refraining from doing things for the conscience of others who are not believers. It's more important to promote Christ than to exercise your freedoms and thereby become a stumbling block to someone else. There's an exchange taking place. It's profitable to forego freedoms for a greater good to be realized.

❤ A PROFITABLE BREAKUP

Remember, profit is gain, advantage, usefulness or expedience. If breaking up with someone, in the long run, puts you at an advantage, was useful or is expedient to accomplishing the will of God in your life, then the break was profitable. Being single now may be expedient to you being married to the glory of God in the future. Perhaps what you're doing in this season will put you in position for God to introduce you to your husband.

Your breakup may be expedient to you finding your purpose. You may be free to participate and pursue things that fulfill you. Now God can use you because you have the advantage of being single. You don't have to make time for God while pursuing this relationship. You are no longer robbing God of your time, tithes or talents for this relationship. You can give those resources back to Him and He can use you in the service of others.

Maybe you were ready to sell your soul in exchange for this relationship and God stepped in to stop the sale. Whatever the reason, know that God can yield a profit from your breakup.

❤ ARE YOU BROKE OR IN DEBT?

Just because you're broke, it doesn't mean you're in debt. Though conventional money wisdom says to pay yourself first, many choose to pay their bills first. They may have little to no money left for themselves. They are broke. However, they don't have debt. They owe no one anything. At the end of the month, they've paid everything they're obligated to pay.

Being spiritually or emotionally broke doesn't mean you are in debt, "upside down", or owe any man anything. It doesn't mean an individual owes you anything. It simply means now is the time to start to build your worth. You're at ground zero.

Being broke doesn't mean broken being repair. Being broke means you don't have any more and that's OK because God gives freely. Maybe you're broke and don't have anything left because you haven't been to God in a while. You haven't been filled up by Him. If this is the case, repent and return to Him. He's ready to fill you up.

ELIMINATING EMOTIONAL DEBT

If you're going to be ready for a relationship, you cannot have significant debt to contend with in any area of your life. There are plenty of examples of people who end relationships and find themselves in financial straits. There are innumerable books or pieces of literature dedicated to the process of getting out of financial debt.

But in a book talking about spiritual and emotional wholeness after a breakup, I feel it's necessary to examine how you can assess and tackle any emotional debt you may have post breakup.

What is emotional debt? How do you incur it?

Debt and credit is about ownership, access, and the ability to acquire. A person is in debt when they spend more than they have. A person in emotional debt may purchase things on credit with the expectation they will have the currency before the bill is due. However, when payment is required, they don't have the means to pay what they owe. This person may put up things they can't afford to lose as collateral and find themselves in bankruptcy.

How do you get out of emotional debt? How do you build a good emotional credit rating? How do you cultivate a positive emotional net worth?

#1: FACE YOUR DEBT

The first thing you need to do is face your debt. You need to read your emotional credit report. You will need to sit down with those you have emotional attachments and relationships with and find out if you owe them.

This is a hard process to undertake. It's difficult to sit silently while friends recount all the times you stood them up or used them. It can hurt to hear your kids say they don't tell you things because they are afraid of your reaction. It can be demoralizing to hear you have shown yourself to be unreliable.

It's important to note some of the items on your report may be out of date. You might want to dispute the debt, or the amount owed. It's OK to ask for more information to gain clarity on what commitments you haven't fulfilled. It's not OK to let defensiveness or avoidance hold you back from getting a clear picture of where your emotional net worth stands.

Understand you are responsible for paying off your debt. Even if others played a part in incurring the debt, you're the one who's culpable for it. You have to answer for what you spent. You're the one who deals with the impairment of a large debt, and you're the one who has to work her way out of it.

You need to figure out exactly what you lost. You can close your eyes and refuse to answer the calls of debt collectors, but the debt will still be there. It will continue to impair you and hamper the things you want to acquire in the future. If you truly want to run the race set before you with perseverance, you are going to have to lay aside the weight of emotional debt. The only way to do this is to confront and address it.

God forgives sin. All we must do is repent and confess. But for some of our relationships with people, more is required. Our poor decisions may have impacted the credit of others who co-signed for us or invested their own emotional capital into our ventures. An admittance of guilt and a commitment to be better may not be enough to wipe out the debt we have incurred. The relationship may be forfeit and unable to be fixed. As much as this knowledge may hurt, we need to know this before we put emotional currency toward a relationship that's been written off.

#2: STOP THROWING GOOD MONEY AFTER BAD

Once you have taken stock of what you owe, you must stop throwing good money after bad. If you spent years investing money and time into a person, if you've forfeited opportunities you wanted to pursue to pour into your relationship, then it may prove difficult to walk away from the investment you've made in the relationship. You might choose to remain friends with your ex or continue a toxic friendship because of what you've already invested. This might not be the best investment of your time, talents, or tender feelings. Perhaps you're throwing good money after bad emotionally by continuing these relationships.

Spending precious time dwelling on the failure or the losses you've suffered only builds your emotional debt. It builds the amount of guilt or shame you have over what you did or didn't do in the relationship. It keeps you angry. Replaying what happened over and over in your head and wondering how it could have been different is counterproductive. All you're doing is wasting energy you could put toward learning from the experience or applying the knowledge you've gained.

It's important to take stock of emotional money pits. If you're still throwing money into things that are broken, you need to sever those connections. It's important. You don't have an extra emotional dollar to spend in the wrong areas. You need to ask yourself the questions that hurt here.

This is more than taking stock of your emotional viability; it's taking stock of your viability as a person—mind, body, and spirit. This is deeper than determining your readiness to date again; it's evaluating what you have available to invest in all your existing and future relationships.

#3: SET UP AN EMOTIONAL EMERGENCY FUND

One thing Dave Ramsey teaches is no matter how much debt you're in, the first thing you must do is set up an emergency fund. Your emergency fund needs to be fully funded first because if anything else happens while you're paying off debt, you will not be able to stay on track without it.

If you invested in someone and the relationship broke up, there are things you'll have to restock and rebuild. There's work to be done to be whole. Sometimes this takes a long time and sometimes it takes no time at all. It's not about how much time you spend; it's about if you're whole again.

How do you put money into your emotional saving account? You build your identity off your relationship with Christ. In your emotional savings account, there should be things tied to your unshakeable identity—your eternal identity. Your relationship with Christ, who you are in Him, and the person He created you to be. Being a healthy representation of a Christian inside and out.

Invest in your relationship with God. Invest in other fulfilling relationships, such as those with family and friends. Invest in hobbies or pursuits that make you happy. These are funds you can draw from when a situation or circumstance requires more than you were prepared to expend on it.

Once your relationship ends and some of the opportunity cost is gone, reinvest your time in fulfilling activities. Invest in skills that will be an asset your future self can draw from should the need arise.

Even though at one point I lost my job, my relationship, my home, the city I lived in and my home church, I still had funds I could draw on. I lost nothing God couldn't give back to me a hundredfold. I didn't lose anything I couldn't afford to lose.

I thought I did at some points. I felt like giving up at certain points. But in those moments, I was able to draw on my emergency fund. That's when girlfriends came alongside me, inviting me on trips, encouraging me to get involved, showing me I'm still a valuable person who's worth pursuing and spending time with. That's when church family stepped in to celebrate me on my birthday, invest in the activities I hosted, and committed to being honest and digging into the hard things with me. All my investments paid dividends which canceled out some of my emotional debt.

#4: START PAYING YOUR EMOTIONAL/SPIRITUAL DEBTS

Sometimes, getting out of emotional debt involves reaching out to old friends and starting from the bottom. You might have to earn their trust and a spot in their schedule. Sometimes it means starting from the bottom with your child or children when you haven't been present in their lives. You might have to allow them to set dates to see you and boundaries for the relationship. You must make on time payments into your relationships before credit is extended to you again. Don't expect to be given credit for trying or the benefit of the doubt when there's a question about your actions. Trust is an emotional currency that must be earned.

Spiritually, you wipe the slate clean through confession and repentance. Think about the transactional language used in The Lord's Prayer. It says, "forgive us of our debts, as we forgive our debtors (Matt. 6:12)." This shows the transactional nature of God forgiving us of a debt we couldn't pay in exchange for us forgiving others who "owe" us. Not only is it mentioned in the Lord's Prayer, it's mentioned again in the same chapter: if we don't forgive we are not forgiven (Matt. 6:14-15).

Your emotional debt is forgiven when you forgive the emotional debt owed to you by others. You can't hold on to what someone owes you.

> [21] Then Peter came up and said to him, "Lord, how often will my brother sin against me, and I forgive him? As many as seven times?" [22] Jesus said to him, "I do not say to you seven times, but seventy-seven times. [23] "Therefore the kingdom of heaven may be compared to a king who wished to settle accounts with his servants. [24] When he began to settle, one was brought to him who owed him ten thousand talents. [25] And since he could not pay, his master ordered him to be sold, with his wife and children and all that he had, and payment to be made. [26] So the servant fell on his knees, imploring him, 'Have patience with me, and I will pay you everything.' [27] And out of pity for him, the master of that servant released him and forgave him the debt. [28] But when that same servant went out, he found one of his fellow servants who owed him a hundred denarii, and seizing him, he began to choke him, saying, 'Pay what you owe.' [29] So his fellow servant fell down and pleaded with him, 'Have patience with me, and

I will pay you.' [30] He refused and went and put him in prison until he should pay the debt. [31] When his fellow servants saw what had taken place, they were greatly distressed, and they went and reported to their master all that had taken place. [32] Then his master summoned him and said to him, 'You wicked servant! I forgave you all that debt because you pleaded with me. [33] And should not you have had mercy on your fellow servant, as I had mercy on you?' [34] And in anger his master delivered him to the jailers, until he should pay all his debt. [35] So also my heavenly Father will do to every one of you, if you do not forgive your brother from your heart." Matt. 18:21-35

#5: REMIND YOURSELF OF THE VALUE OF BEING DEBT FREE

It may not seem as if your payments are making a dent in the great debt you owe, but don't stop making them. Remind yourself of the value of being debt free.

Temptations will come. There will be enticements designed to distract you or pull you off track. There are any number of ways to spend your emotional capital. It's up to you to stay focused on your goal.

#6: KEEP INVESTING IN YOUR SAVINGS

When you enter a new romantic relationship, don't let your other relationships wither away. Stay in contact with your friends. Spend time with them. Continue pursuing hobbies and activities that make you a better version of yourself. Don't cease to cultivate non-romantic attachments when you find a romantic partner.

This is called diversifying your portfolio. Investing is good, but all our money shouldn't be in investments, and all our emotional and spiritual currency shouldn't either. We need to continue to build up our savings. Savings accounts keep what we put in and bear interest without incurring loss.

One secure investment you can make is in your relationship with Christ. Other relationships can lose their value. The people you invest in can fail to deliver. They can leave you emotionally bankrupt. Your investment in following Jesus and being obedient to Him will always yield a return. It will always bear interest.

EMOTIONAL INVESTMENT

In high school, I took a summer class on investing. I was given an imaginary $50,000 to invest in stocks. I had to check the performance of my stocks each morning in the newspaper and record their progress.

My selection process for stocks was simple. I chose to invest in companies with products I used and loved. Though I never invested real money in their stocks, I bought more meals at the restaurants and shopped more often at the stores I chose for the project. I was mentally invested in the success of the brand, if not financially. I saw my purchases as contributing to their success.

The performance of my stocks didn't directly affect my grade. I was able to switch my investments three times during this six-week period, but I never did. When I chose, I committed.

Checking the stocks each day became the barometer for my mood. If my stock was performing well, my day started off well. If my stocks were down, I was down. I didn't receive a dividend check or benefit financially in any way, yet I was as emotionally invested in the stock market as any hardcore investor.

At the end of the summer, I left the Horizons-Upward Bound program with less money than I came with, not because my stocks performed badly, but because I hadn't made any real investments. The money I came with was spent on candy, soda, slices of pizza, and cute pens. The fantasy of being a stock market investor was over, and it had profited me nothing.

Women all over the world have had experiences like my summer learning the stock market in their romantic relationships. Some of them are mentally and emotionally invested in relationships, but they're investment is symbolic at best. They haven't invested any real relationship currency or capital into their partner or the relationship. Although she may not know the agony of losing big on a genuine investment, this woman experiences the same frustration and pain of an investment not paying off like she'd hoped.

Relationships require investment. It's risky to invest our hard-earned capital into another person or relationship, but without risk, there's no reward. Here are a few tips on emotional investment to better equip you to evaluate investment opportunities, make real investments, and work in good faith toward a profitable partnership with someone.

INVESTMENT INVITES RISK AS WELL AS REWARD

If profit is advantage, investment is risk. You must decide if you're willing to take that risk and invest. If you choose not to invest, you won't experience true loss, but you also can't reap a real reward.

Before entering another relationship, ask yourself: What is going to be your level of investment in relationships going forward? Will you back the investment with currency the two of you can use to build a successful partnership, or will you be pretend investing like me in my summer program? Will you let your emotional involvement become an investment the other person benefits from?

♥ INVESTMENT REQUIRES CURRENCY

You can't make an investment without currency. You must have something of value you can put into the relationship. **There is no true investment without currency.** It doesn't matter if you see yourself as mentally or emotionally invested; if the other person doesn't experience an influx of currency, you will see no growth or dividends.

Social media has made it easy for women to overinvest emotionally in men they don't have a real relationship with. Their only real investment is social media follows and tagging them in posts like #mancrushmonday. It's a sad day when these women scroll down their #MCM's timeline and see he's in a relationship or married. They can be just as hurt as a woman who was in a relationship with him. But these women had no real investment in this man, and no relationship with him.

Many think they are making significant investments with emotional currency when they are not. They have no clue what constitutes currency in emotional matters. Social media likes or comments don't constitute currency. Emotional currency consists of the time, energy, expertise, connections, money, and other tangible contributions you make to a person or relationship.

We've all experienced relationships in which someone says they are invested in us and our success, but they haven't invested any capital. They put nothing into us, yet they expect a piece of the profits. These are the individuals who will tell others their relationship with us and try to get some residual shine from our accomplishments.

There are plenty of people who will give you advice. They'll tell you what you need to do to be more profitable. They'll invent reasons why they deserve a share of your profits.

No one likes these individuals. These people are the worst. They anger and irritate us. Yet, if we're honest, many of us have been this person. It's especially easy to be this person in romantic relationships.

Maybe you didn't make an investment in your previous relationship. Maybe you were the person who contributed opinions instead of currency to the other person's bottom line. You may have received some of the profits the other person generated. But without true investment, it's easy to exit. There's something about when you invest in something that makes you want to work hard to see it succeed.

If you don't put up the currency, you cannot claim the dividends. It didn't matter how closely I watched the stock market in the summer program; I would never profit from my investment.

True investment is not a spectator sport. If you're going to be tied emotionally and mentally to a person's performance, put some currency where your sentiment resides. When you invest real emotional currency in a relationship, you will work to bring about a specific outcome or turn a profit because you have something to lose.

♥ BUYING WHAT SOMEONE IS SELLING IS NOT AN INVESTMENT

Investment involves a much more substantial commitment of currency than a like on social media or a one-time purchase. It requires looking past what you may want in the present and seeing what you can have a hand in building for the future.

While I thought I was investing in companies by buying meals or products from them, my purchases had little to do with the performance of their stock. While profits are considered in stock prices, an individual purchase is miniscule in comparison to what the brand brings in during a quarter. Additionally, stocks go up or down based on profit forecasts, announcements of new advancements/products, jobs' reports, and a slew of other factors in addition to goods and services sold.

More importantly, an individual does not get a share in the profits for buying a product. The only purchases that will pay dividends are purchases of the company's stock. Stockholders own a share of the company and will receive a percentage of the profits based on the amount of shares they own.

It's OK to buy someone's product without investing in their company's stock. You might need what they have for sale, but not want to invest in the company. There's nothing wrong with this type of exchange if both parties know what they are giving and getting.

Don't lead anyone on about your level of investment, and don't invest with anyone without knowing what you can expect to receive. If all you're doing is buying goods or services, don't be jealous or envious of others who do invest when they reap their dividends. The brand, or the person, owes you nothing you did not pay for.

♥ LOYALTY NEEDS TO BE EARNED

A potential investment should prove its value and potential for profit. A good investment is profitable now, and on its current trajectory, can expect healthy growth and profits in the future. There are plenty of people you like or who can be useful that won't meet these requirements. You can still have a relationship with and invest in these people, but it's important to extend your loyalty to those relationships that are more likely to endure.

When deciding whether to extend your loyalty to someone

you've invested in, you must consider who they are right now. What is the current profit of this relationship? Is this man a good Christian **now**? Does he display the qualities of a good father **now**?

Potential is important, but there's a degree to which potential must be proven. Past performance is the best predictor of future performance. Has this person fulfilled the potential they had previously? Don't get distracted playing the exceptions game.

An investment's current performance is a good starting place for evaluating how loyal you should be to it, but it's not the only factor. Investors know the stock market is a long game. Whatever you ascribe loyalty to must not outlive its growth potential and usefulness. Like any long-term investment, stocks fluctuate over time. You want to invest in stock that will reward your loyalty.

Once loyalty is extended, it isn't shaken by the ups and downs of life. The day to day fluctuations are unimportant. What matters is what you have when you cash out.

Some people were financially devastated in the housing market crash in the mid to late 2000s, while others are now living well off investments made or maintained during this time. Those who were able to invest while buy-ins were low and/or stay in until the market recovered are reaping the rewards of their loyalty.

The same is true in relationships. The daily fluctuations aren't the focus. Building up the brand, honoring your investments, making further investments wisely, and making your moves with the long game in mind are the focal points.

Relationship investments aren't the same as investments in the stock market, but many of the principles parallel each other. We must be cognizant of what constitutes true investment, and we must be intentional about the relationships we invest in if we want to have mutually beneficial relationships.

As discussed in "The Breaks," much of the brokenness a person suffers in a bad breakup can be due to broken expectations. The person thinks they know what they signed up for and find they are wrong. It's important to know what's required of you to achieve the results you want. Many women have been broken when an investment tanks and the debt for their decision is collected. Many have lost assets they didn't know were put up as collateral—virginity, integrity, trust, etc.

Before you make an investment, you must ask yourself, "Can I afford to lose what I'm investing?" This is not to harden your heart or curb your willingness to invest in relationships; it's to help you understand the import of what you're doing.

Not all investments produce a profit. Your emotional capital is a precious commodity. Use it wisely.

All relationships are risky and come at a cost emotionally, spiritually, financially, and/or in time and opportunities. You will need to invest trust, time, and energy into them. What's a good return on such an investment? What do you expect from the other person?

Often, expectations are uncommunicated and therefore unmet. By not acknowledging and communicating the expected outcome of an investment, many women (and men) enter relationships that are incapable of yielding the returns they require. If the individual had communicated what they were willing to invest and what they wanted in return, this incompatibility could have been discovered and avoided.

All relationships don't have to be major investments. Some are purchases or trades. They provide us with goods or services we need at a cost we're willing to pay. It's our responsibility to know the difference. We must know what each level of investment requires from us and what the other person is prepared to give in the exchange. Investments are risky, but they are worth the reward if we invest wisely.

Don't be *surprised* when your " *cheat day* "

becomes a " *cheat week* " and eventually a " *cheat life* "

where the *only* person

being *cheated*

is *you.*

Emotional Health

MANY WOMEN FOCUS ON THEIR HEALTH and fitness when working through the aftermath of a breakup. They may start a new diet or exercise regimen for self-improvement or to show their ex what they've lost. Getting stronger and healthier physically is empowering. It can repair and restore a woman's self-esteem and confidence.

A focus on physical health and fitness is admirable, but women seeking to be made whole inside and out must pay attention to their emotional and spiritual health and fitness as well. Physical, mental, spiritual and emotional health are intertwined. Sickness in one sphere tends to manifest itself in another. The woman desiring wholeness must seek the healing of her entire being—body, mind, and soul.

Jesus understood this well. His miraculous healings weren't limited to people with physical ailments. He healed people possessed of demons as well as lepers and lame men. He restored the dead to life because of His compassion for the loved ones left suffering. A God like this would not leave a woman alone to deal with her heartache, nor would He want her to settle for the poor substitute of a partial wholeness when true wholeness is available.

Up to this point, several symptoms of emotional and spiritual illness have been examined. Many issues that grow out of inner brokenness have been discussed. Now it's time to dig deep into the idea of emotional and spiritual health. You've separated yourself from your ex and rested in God's truth about who you are, but you can't run the race set before you with perseverance until you lay aside the sins and weight that so easily beset you (Heb. 12:1 KJV).

What constitutes a healthy disposition mentally, spiritually, and emotionally? What is emotional junk food, and how do you avoid its empty calories? How do you stop indulging in negative self-talk or address addiction? Should you take emotional cheat days?

YOU ARE WHAT YOU EAT

What you consume is important to your health. Most women try to put healthy foods into their bodies and exercise on a regular basis. However, as days fall into predictable rhythms, many drift away from their health goals. They eat more fast food or microwave meals and consume them later than they should. The number on the scale or the fit of their clothes shocks them out of their stupor and makes them wonder how they could have fallen so far off course.

What happened is easy to see. They chose fast and convenient over wholesome and nutritious. They chose not to go for a walk or make it to an exercise class at the gym. Women confronted with the effects of their inattention often turn to fast fixes like fad diets and cleanses to take the weight off without realizing lasting results come from changing their lifestyle.

Whether a break up makes you want to raid the refrigerator or rids you of your appetite, what you choose to do is your choice. Pain, like all feelings, is merely information. You decide how you respond to the information.

Has your mental, spiritual, and emotional health rebounded from your breakup? If you're still working your way back to health, following these principles will inspire lasting change.

♥ Stop Consuming Emotional Junk Food

Emotional junk food consists of thought processes, information, and advice which seems to satisfy or fill a need in the moment but has no nutritional value for your mind or soul. It might make you feel better, but it has no basis in the rightly divided word of God. You may enjoy consuming it, but afterward, you feel gross, heavy, lethargic, or tired.

It's easy to become addicted to the sweet taste or energy boost provided by social media, gossip, self-help books, or positive affirmations. You may find you can't make it through your day without scrolling your feed or repeating a few phrases with deliberate alliteration to keep you from crashing.

Beware. The more you indulge, the more emotional weight creeps on. Soon you've packed on envy, jealousy, wrath, strife, slander, backbiting, selfish ambition, greed, low-self-esteem, fear of failure, comparison, discontentment, depression, etc.

Media is not the only form of emotional junk food you could be consuming. Some of your relationships may serve the same purpose. You may continue a relationship with a friend or potential mate you feel like you are better than because it makes you feel pride or gives you a sense of accomplishment. Conversely, you may maintain a relationship with someone who makes you feel worse about yourself to self-flagellate. The jealousy and envy of some women becomes exaggerated because they insist on remaining connected to people who inspire these feelings in them.

Media, social media, books, positive sayings, and relationships aren't inherently bad. You may not be using any of these as an emotional equivalent to a pint of ice cream or bar of chocolate. But if you are, it's time to sever your connection with these things and develop some fruit of the spirit.

A breakup may cause you to consume a ton of emotional junk food and put on a large amount of emotional weight. Like physical weight gain, emotional weight can make you feel awkward in social situations and in relationships because you don't feel confident or comfortable in your skin. Unfortunately, it's a lot harder to find a garment that covers this up.

The best way to stop repeating an old habit is to replace it with a new one. Instead of consuming empty calories that don't provide satisfaction, consume the word. The word is described as bread, milk, meat, and water—healthy, filling things.

♥ Quit Indulging in Negative Self-Talk

Many women wrestle with negative self-talk daily. They speak critically to themselves. They expect to fail. Failure in any form reinforces the idea they are failures. The negative self-talk slowly takes over until it's the only conversation these women have with themselves.

Some women put themselves down for being "emotional." They try to dismiss any feelings they have. Some will even attempt to use the bible to justify ignoring feelings. However, the bible doesn't support their position. The bible doesn't advocate avoiding or ignoring feelings; it urges us to confront our feelings. The word of God gives a diagnosis and provides the prescription to cure what ails the child of God, even their feelings. But to get the remedy, you must acknowledge the symptoms and see the physician.

The bible doesn't say don't feel; it gives the correct course of action for dealing with emotions. Be angry and sin not (Eph. 4:26). Forgive those who have trespassed against you. If you have ought against your brother, tell them their fault (Matt. 18:15). Don't worry about anything, but instead, pray about everything (Phil. 4:6 NLT). In other words, when you feel worry, pray. Any anxiety you have didn't originate with God, but you can leave it with Him through prayer.

The bible addresses where feelings come from. God didn't give you a spirit of fear, but of power, love and self-control (2 Tim. 1:7). Feelings have a spiritual origin. They can be brought under the power of God and forced to submit.

Having feelings isn't the problem. Feelings indicate whose spirit is at work in you. They identify areas you have and haven't submitted to the will of God. They mark growth and degeneration. As I said before, feelings are information. This knowledge can be powerful. Rightly applied, it becomes wisdom.

People in the bible have feelings, and they express them to God. One example of this is David. David has an intimate relationship with the LORD. The Psalms of David, along with the recounting of his life in I & II Samuel, I Kings, and I Chronicles, portray David as a man unafraid to pour out his feelings to the Lord. No matter the feeling or the object of those feelings, David is open and honest with the Lord about them. David is an emotional person, yet he is called a man after God's own heart (1 Sam. 13:14; Acts 13:22).

Psalm 51 is a golden chapter for those seeking words to express the feelings of guilt, anguish and repentance associated with sin. David has sinned with Bathsheba and killed her husband Uriah before being confronted by the prophet Nathan. David begs God not to cast him away from His presence or take His spirit back. He's hurt. He's afraid of what God thinks of him or might do to him. He's broken and contrite. He's in anguish over this sin he's committed.

David constantly positioned himself in relationship to God. He considered how God would feel about his actions, whether he felt justified in his actions or not. He made his feelings submit to what God said, not by refusing to acknowledge them, but by bringing them into the light and asking God to give him a clean heart and renew a right spirit within him.

If you're engaging in negative self-talk, bring those feelings to the Lord. Cast your cares upon Him because He cares for you (1 Pet. 5:7). Fill yourself with truth about who you are in Christ. Force your feelings to submit to the word of God instead of allowing them to defeat you.

♥ Don't Cheat Yourself with Cheat Days

I don't like the term "cheat day." Cheating has a connotation of guilt and doing something wrong. I don't like the concept of a cheat day, a day where you give yourself permission to indulge (and often, overindulge) in things you've denied yourself for a week. It's positioned as a big hurrah before you're back on the diet again. People slog through the week while looking forward to the day they can cheat on their diet. This is a setup for failure.

By giving certain days a connotation of illicitness, or freedom to give in to temptation, you make them more attractive than other days. In popular culture today, sin has become synonymous with sexy. An action being "wrong" or taboo is alluring. People tend to indulge in the taboo, even though they know their actions will result in guilt and shame, especially if someone finds out.

They might beat themselves up and wonder why they can't stop falling into the same temptations over and over. They might conclude this sin is part of who they are. They become addicted to the rush of feeling like they got away with something without realizing the high price they're paying for the thrill. They're chipping away at their core beliefs to pay for their illicit "fun."

As Christians, the core of who we are and what we do is comprised of the knowledge Christ died for us, and we are to live for Him. We have put on Christ. The Holy Spirit dwells in us and walks with us on the narrow way that leads us to our home with the Lord.

You will find theologians who push the concepts of grace and forgiveness while brushing aside holiness as legalistic and a false doctrine. Holiness isn't as attractive as grace and won't draw as many crowds. Many "teachers" and "preachers" try to convince believers that they don't need to be holy. They teach repentance as if it's interchangeable with apology. "As long as you're sorry, God will forgive you." They abuse the scripture to influence emotions and scratch itching ears. But the word of God hasn't changed regarding holiness.

The Hebrews writer instructed Christians to spur one another on to love and good works (Heb. 10:24). God said be holy as I am holy several times in Leviticus, and Peter repeats the call to holiness (1 Pet. 1:15-16). I don't see any wiggle room in faith without works is dead (James 2:26). A branch connected to the true vine will have the evidence of fruit. Those branches that don't are cut off and thrown into the fire (John 15:2, 5-6). You don't get to give yourself all the grace and refuse the call to be holy.

The world encourages people to play chicken with their salvation. The unwary person will strive to cram in as many sinful pleasures as he can get away with before he decides to settle down, become responsible and really live for the Lord.

Christians can even fall into this trap. Some who profess to know Christ still operate on the cheat day model. They sneak and do things they shouldn't every now and then. But the thing is, when a person positions sin as an attractive indulgence to look forward to, they become more and more inclined to indulge on "non-cheat" days.

If you schedule sin, don't be surprised when your "cheat day" becomes a "cheat week" and eventually a "cheat life" where the only person being cheated is you. Understand you're not getting away with anything. You can't fool a scale when you cheat on your diet; what makes you think you're fooling God when you cheat on Him?

♥ Address Addiction

Addiction plays a role in the consumption of emotional junk food and cheat days, but its effects on health is extend much further. Addictions alter you mentally, physically, financially, emotionally and spiritually. They leave their mark on every area of your life.

Addictions decide what relationships stay or go in an addict's life. It will drive a wedge between the addict and anyone who holds them accountable. Addicts will begin to avoid the people who recognize the signs of addiction and call them out on them. Over time, the people closest to an addict will be those most accepting of her behavior.

Because addictions rob addicts of their sense of time passing, it's difficult for them to keep commitments. Gamblers, alcoholics, compulsive shoppers, and porn addicts get lost in the vortex of watching and doing. All the while, time to repent and change is slipping unnoticed through their fingers.

There are things the bible tells us to flee and turn away from. We would do well to heed these warnings. If you've fallen into the grip of addiction of any kind, seek help. Gather supportive people around you. Sin and addiction thrive on isolation. They want to double team you, to keep you under their control. But Christ came to set the captive free. Grab hold to the freedom you have in Christ.

LOSE WAIT

Some women pick up "wait" in their relationships. They're waiting until their relationship matures into an engagement, marriage, or the next logical step to do a, b, or c. Wait gain can creep on stealthily and go unnoticed until it's clear what the woman is waiting for will never happen.

Gaining wait can have the same effect emotionally as gaining weight physically—poor self-esteem, shame, self-medicating, regret, and depression. Other people might see the wait gain and know it's unhealthy, but until the woman herself is willing to acknowledge it, there's nothing they can do to help her.

I can think of several instances in my relationship where I picked up wait. I thought it was healthy wait. I believed I was investing in a shared future with this person. I likened it to building muscle. In reality, my joints ached from walking through life carrying excess wait.

If you spent your entire relationship waiting, you may be beginning to realize how weighed down you are by the wait you've picked up. You can continue to make excuses for it, or you can begin working to rid yourself of it. You might not know where to begin. What plan should you follow? How do you measure success?

Wait loss, like weight loss, is a personal journey. There's no "one size fits all" plan that will help you achieve your goals. What works for me might not work for you.

Whatever you decide on, know you won't reach your goal wait overnight. This is going to take commitment and effort. You owe it to yourself to be persistent and consistent in your regimen.

Wait loss requires two things: a change of diet—what you consume—and exercise. No matter what changes you would like to make, these two facets must be considered. What you allow into your heart and mind is what will come out. The muscles you use are the ones that will strengthen.

You may have several different "problem areas" you want to tighten, strengthen, or improve. An area you might want to lose some wait in is in your home or location. If you were waiting to get married to buy a house or settle in a city, state, or country, you may focus on losing wait in this area. You may begin this process by consuming more information about the area you want to live in or attending homebuyers' workshops. You might take trips to the city where you want to relocate, visiting churches or interviewing for positions in the area.

If you were waiting to pursue a different career, you could take a class or volunteer to accrue knowledge or experience in the field. You might want to pursue hobbies in your free time. Your hobby might turn into a moneymaking venture, or it might remain a release for you, which is equally important.

Lastly, your wait loss journey may include getting more involved in your local church. You can start attending Sunday school faithfully, visiting the sick, fellowshipping with others after church, participating in a life group or bible study, or getting involved with a ministry.

Don't sit on things because you're waiting for your happily ever after. Your life is happening **now,** and it deserves to be recorded, shared, and experienced to the fullest **now,** while you're waiting.

Your life is waiting on you. Experience it. Live it. Do it. Stop waiting for what you think you need to be listened to, accepted, or appreciated. Don't worry about being mocked for standing on your convictions or sharing your opinion before you have certain credentials. Lose the wait.

GAIN WAIT

There is wait to be gained from a breakup. When you break up with someone, the relationship clock is reset. There's additional time added to the date you could possibly get married, have children, or share your load with a life partner.

You will need to gain patience in this season. You will need to exercise your discernment and wisdom, to build these muscles up. Don't be misled; gaining wait can be just as difficult as losing wait. It can also be just as rewarding.

When my relationship ended I let go of several waits, but I also had to gain some wait. For example, I'm 33. I had to let go of the idea of being married by 33 and pick up wait. I have to wait to do couples' activities I look forward to, like attending special events with my hand in the crook of my significant other's arm or resting my head on his shoulder while watching a movie.

Wait is gained the same way it is lost. It requires a focus on diet and exercise. Healthy wait gain requires you to eat more frequently. You don't consume spiritual junk food calories to bulk up; instead, you feast on the word consistently. You don't avoid exercise, but you exercise strategically to achieve your desired result.

THE MOST IMPORTANT HEALTH TIP

> [12] Not as though I had already attained, either were already perfect: but I follow after, if that I may apprehend that for which also I am apprehended of Christ Jesus. [13] Brethren, I count not myself to have apprehended: but this one thing I do, forgetting those things which are behind, and reaching forth unto those things which are before, [14] I press toward the mark for the prize of the high calling of God in Christ Jesus. Phil. 3:12-14

In Philippians, Paul writes about his efforts to apprehend, or capture and understand, the reason for which God grabbed hold of him. The way Paul approaches this goal is to forget what's behind him, reach for what's before him, and press toward the mark he wants to achieve. Paul let go of what was behind Him to reach for what was in front of him. He pressed forward to obtain.

This should be your focus as a single woman who's healed and whole: to let go of the past and to reach and press for what God has for you.

The singular focus of your single life should be fixed on pleasing God. What I see in breakups is a tendency to turn the focus off the relationship and onto self. Women want to make sure they aren't rehearsing the hurts that happened to them again and again. They seek to rid themselves of every issue they believe is holding them back from moving forward.

It's important to make sure you aren't internalizing or overthinking in emotionally unhealthy ways, but you must be careful not to make yourself the object of your focus. You cannot heal yourself, no matter how much time you take to focus on yourself. Fix your focus where it should have been, where it should always be—on God.

What would you tell yourself / someone struggling with a break up?

Be gentle with yourself. It's hard, and it's okay to be sad and disappointed, but don't stay there. Feel the feelings and acknowledge them, process them with safe and loving people, and then choose to place your hope in God, and not your circumstances (honestly, I'm preaching this to myself right now, too!).

I would also say to keep seeking God with all of your heart. Use your pain and your frustration to push you even closer to Him. Cling to Him! And pour out your heart to Him, too...don't be afraid to let Him know exactly how you feel and let Him know how much you need Him.

♥ Katie H.

I would tell myself to be confident. I am a daughter of a king and I deserve better. I would tell myself to walk away when it doesn't feel right in your gut. Usually, when there is smoke, there is fire and this man convinced me nothing was burning, even though I knew it.

I would tell others to trust that God has better for us. He won't

leave us or forsake us ever! He is working to make all things good.
♥ Kacy S.

My advice for anyone going through a breakup is to just take it one day at a time. Just focus on making it through that day, because sometimes the heartbreak is so big that it is hard to imagine months or even years down the road.

Use it as a time to really depend on the Lord for everything. It feels like you hit rock bottom and in those moments is when we are most ready to cling to God for everything.

Lastly, you will eventually get over it. It won't hurt forever, and you will understand God's plan eventually. You will see how it all fits in His plan one day.
♥ Natalie M.L.

I would go back and tell myself this is God's plan and if you don't accept it right away, it will eat you up mentally. I guess I would say the same thing to anyone else struggling because I know from experience. It won't be easy to get out of the mental stronghold, so it's best to accept it immediately so it doesn't happen to you.
♥ Ayanna S.

If I could go back and tell myself one thing after my breakup, it's that things are going to work out, it's okay to not understand, and that God has a hold of my heart.

For someone currently struggling with a breakup, I would tell them that they will be able to move on, even though it may not seem like it. They will get back to their old self. Better days are ahead. Sometimes our deepest hurts may be our biggest blessings in disguise.
♥ Erica U.

It'll work out. It'll be okay. It seems like the entire world is crumbling around you (and maybe it is), but I promise you it WILL start to settle down + go back to a new normal.

As painful as this part of the story is, don't throw it away. You might learn more in the breakup than you did during the relationship, so write it all down. Journal your heart out; it's therapeutic for you now and encouraging for you to read later.

❤ Kelsey Baldwin, Owner, Paper + Oats

I would advise to pray, study God's word, pray, seclude yourself from worldly distractions, pray, and find a few close, intimate friends you can be transparent with and pour your soul out to them and God. Continue this cycle until you have some peace and remember it for someone else who will need it. Be there for them.

❤ Cheryl S.

I would go back and remind myself that all things work together for the good, for those who love the Lord and are called according to His purpose.

❤ Andreana J.

I would tell myself to take time for ME. The relationship after my divorce lasted for 10 months and it crushed me probably even more than the divorce simply because I was broken when that relationship started. You can't be in a relationship when one or both are broken.

After that one I took a full year to myself and was the happiest I had EVER been. I never realized how important it is to take time alone and work through every single emotion on my own without another party involved or swaying me one way or another. I had never been stronger than after being alone for a year...

Think about why it didn't work out and to try to focus on the negative rather than the positive. The more straight forward you are with yourself the quicker you will learn your worth and how much better off you are without the toxicity of the bad relationship.

I would also advise there is nothing wrong with therapy, it's a necessity at times and can help tremendously.

And lastly, I did a "100 days of happy" which was just taking a picture of one thing every day that made me happy whether it was the clouds in the sky, a really good coffee, or a person...I made myself find one happy each and every day.

♥ Nichole H.

My "Dear You" Letter

November 9, 2017, I wrote a letter to November 9, 2016 Erica. This letter was everything I would want to tell myself in the immediate aftermath of my breakup. Below is an excerpt from the letter I wrote, something I think any woman going through a breakup needs to hear.

> God made you strong and kind, not in a moment, but in your marrow. Life has knocked you down time after time... and yet you get up gracefully... You think you were weak because you had to ask God to give you the strength to do what you know you needed to do, but that's what makes you so strong. This strength and kindness aren't momentary aberrations but inherited traits in written into your spiritual DNA. God's strength is made perfect in your weakness has never been more real to...it will never be a scripture you say without intimate knowledge of its truth. God is going to keep showing up strong and kind in your life, and He's going to keep showing you how to be those things, too.
>
> Right now, you're wondering if you're going to shrink back into your shell or harden you heart against love. I can tell you the opposite is true. As you begin to fill your free time serving others, the dams are going to burst, and you are going to find your capacity to give and receive love is so much greater than you ever imagined. You'll find the more you pour out, the more you have to give. In this moment it feels like your heart is a drain and love is rushing out of you like a river, but trust me, it gets better...

let us *run*

with *endurance*

the *race*

that is

set before us,

Hebrews 12:1

Ready for Love

How, when did you decide it was time to start dating again?

I'm just now reaching that point (and still figuring it out, to be honest), but I'm trying to be cautious and continue to heal where I need to heal, but also be open to any opportunities God may bring my way. I don't want to be scared to open my heart again, but I also don't want to just jump into something without allowing myself the time and space needed to heal.

♥ Katie H.

I am casually dating again. It has been 3 months, but I really am not sure it is the right time to start dating again. I'd like to focus more on my relationship with God and myself before I am ready again. I want to learn the lessons God has for me.

I am working on making sure I am refined, and my heart is more like God's. In my past relationships, I had a tendency to overreact sometimes and honestly now I am dealing with trust issues. I am hoping in my future relationships, the man I am with doesn't make me feel like I need to snoop. I pray he doesn't lie and is honest with me.

♥ Kacy S.

I wanted to start dating again about 2 years later. It's now been 6 years and I've only dated about twice since...both who I knew weren't the one for me because they weren't in God like I was.

♥ Ayanna S.

I don't think I was old enough or mature enough to be able to make that decision with a pure heart. I didn't want anything to do with boys for a couple months after the breakup. I was really hard on myself and beat myself up after the breakup, saying I wouldn't date again for a long time and that I would never open up to another guy. Other guys came around, and even though there was interest on both sides it was a kinda messy situation for me.

I was aware of my struggle of wanting to be emotionally attached to someone and find my security in them, but fighting the temptation to fall into that.

♥ Erica U.

I didn't start dating again for about 2 years (mainly because I was pregnant, then had the baby, and then moved to a new city).

There were a few factors that told me I was ready to date again:

1) I was pregnant when he asked for a divorce, so I didn't have to brain capacity to even think about dating until my daughter was born and well out of the newborn phase!

2) I was getting ready to move out of state, so wasn't interested in dating before that.

3) I just felt ready! I don't know how to describe it. I was well out

of love with my ex and wanted that companionship again once my life had settled down with my daughter and the move.
💜 Kelsey B.

I didn't know it was time. I was just trying online dating for the sake of something different. When "R" found me, I knew this was something different. We are blessed to have each other. He is a really good friend and I absolutely see a future with him. I am so thankful for every minute we spend together. He is a good man who works hard and lives simply.
💜 Cheryl S.

Before my last relationship, I was in a season of preparation. I felt like God was showing me a lot about myself and putting me in position to learn a lot about marriage.

When my ex walked into my life, I was convinced that he was the one, but deep down inside I knew I wasn't ready to transition out of [the preparation] season. I needed to keep still, but rather I was swept off my feet. Little did I know, him sweeping me off my feet would land me right on my back.

Before meeting the man of my prayers now, I knew that my season of finding myself, and learning to love myself was over. I was ready to receive whomever God seen fit for me. I had to ensure that I received total healing from my last breakup and that the next would not be a rebound. I also prayed and checked with God on the matter and from that point, I stayed crazy busy in His kingdom until He saw fit for me to meet someone new.
💜 Andreana J.

The

purpose of *discipline:*

to *validate* our status

as *heirs of God,*

develop us,

and *train* us.

Emotional Fitness

There are two components to emotional fitness: eating right and exercising. What we consume is only part of the equation. To be truly fit, we must also exercise.

The bible uses examples of physical exercise to illustrate spiritual concepts, particularly in the story of Jacob's wrestling (Gen. 32:22-32) and Paul's writings. Living a spiritual life is likened to running a race and fighting.

> 24 Do you not know that in a race all the runners run, but only one receives the prize? So run that you may obtain it. 25 Every athlete exercises self-control in all things. They do it to receive a perishable wreath, but we an imperishable. 26 So I do not run aimlessly; I do not box as one beating the air. 27 But I discipline my body and keep it under control, lest after preaching to others I myself should be disqualified. 1 Cor. 9:24-27

The Hebrew writer also talks about running the race:

> Therefore, since we are surrounded by so great a cloud of witnesses, let us also lay aside every weight, and sin which clings so closely, and let us run with endurance the race that is set before us, Hebrews 12:1

Paul addresses the end of his life in these terms in his second letter to Timothy:

> [7] I have fought the good fight, I have finished the race, I have kept the faith. [8] Henceforth there is laid up for me the crown of righteousness, which the Lord, the righteous judge, will award to me on that day, and not only to me but also to all who have loved his appearing. 2 Tim. 4:7-8

All these scriptures use physical exercise or exertion to illustrate how the Christian is to live. Each verse speaks of the discipline and endurance necessary to complete this Christian journey. They also underline the fact the Christian is exerting themselves to obtain the prize, the crown. Everyone who has breathe is called to run the race of life, but not all are running like they are trying to obtain the prize.

In this chapter, you will be called upon to examine your fitness in several ways. You will unpack the need for emotional personal training and discipline and learn to pace yourself, build emotional strength and muscle, and test your fitness.

EMOTIONAL PERSONAL TRAINING

Six months before her wedding, my roommate Tasha decided to take advantage of a free fitness assessment at the gym she belonged to. She invited me along as her guest. Our first meeting with Ron, the trainer, went well. Ron was generous with compliments and careful to stress personal training would only enhance our beauty. Tasha and I cracked jokes and laughed the entire time. You'd never guess less than 24 hours later I'd be taking a knee in the middle of a squash court about to cry, die or both.

The assessment began just like any other fitness assessment. Ron took our measurements, gave me a stern look for forgetting my food journal worksheet, and sent us off for warm up cardio. After fifteen minutes of the treadmill and elliptical, we met Ron on the squash court for a sample personal training session.

Less than thirty seconds in, I was convinced Ron was trying to kill me. He went right into a set of three "fifteen second" wall sits. Those quotation marks are there because Ron kept conveniently "forgetting" how to count.

Instead of switching to another body part to give my burning thighs a break, he switched to lunges. He wanted us to lunge the length of the squash court and back. My thighs cried with every lowered knee. Tasha took big steps and passed me while I struggled to perfectly execute each lunge. My breathing became labored. My legs were shaking.

"I can't do this!" I gasped. I stopped, taking a knee like a punt returner who decides not to run it back. My gaze, and that knee, drilled holes in the court. I was spent. I didn't have anything else.

"You can do this, Erica. Don't quit on me!"

Why not? Why do I always have to be the one to persevere? Why can't I ever throw in the towel? This isn't even my PT appointment. I don't even have a membership to this gym. I thought about all the times I'd given up on myself, on taking care of myself as I knew I should. I thought about all the things I'd failed to complete or hang on to recently. I thought about all the times I was let go, dismissed, or pronounced inadequate. I was failing a fitness assessment. I knew it wasn't possible, but that's what I felt.

I huffed out a breath and tried to stand. "Here, lean on me." I looked up into Ron's big brown eyes. He had met me in the middle of the court. He offered me an arm like a gentleman at a debutante ball. "I'm right here with you."

I expected to see sympathy, or worse, pity, reflected in his eyes. I saw neither. I saw a calm confidence I could do something I was no longer used to doing: fighting through and finishing the hard thing.

I saw his belief in what he had said: "You can do this, Erica. I'm right here with you."

I pulled myself up using his arm for stability. I stepped forward and eased back down.

"There you go! Come on, just three more." Ron's gentle encouragement fell like misty rain on my bent head.

"Good. Come on, two more."

"OK, last one...Good job."

When Ron helped me out of the last wobbly lunge, I wasn't at the end of the squash court. I fell short.

"Alright girl, good job!" Tasha called from the sidelines where she sat catching her breath.

"Good job? I couldn't even finish the exercise." Tears gathered in my eyes for the second time in as many minutes.

"That's OK," Ron said. "This is just the start. You're going to get better."

I tried to scoff, but it turned into a sniff.

We finished the session and headed back to Ron's desk. He was no longer the cute younger trainer at the gym. He was a professional, talking rates and number of sessions. But in the middle of the squash court, he had been the former fat kid who saw where I was and **got it**.

He'd probably been down on one knee with a tough love trainer yelling at him. He'd probably felt his body stop responding to his brain in the middle of a hard workout. More than likely, he'd sat in a similar moment where he realized how far off the path he'd gone, how bad it had gotten. His body had failed him and shown him he wasn't where his mind assured him he was. The scales had fallen off his eyes.

In that moment, my moment holding on to the end of a fast fraying rope, Ron seemed to know I didn't need sympathy, pity or tough love; I needed help. I needed someone to come back for me. I needed someone to be in the fight with me, to let me lean on them.

Ron did things for me and said things to me the man I was dating hadn't done or said, that no one had done or said for a long time. He affirmed me, encouraged me, and partnered with me. Moreover, he allowed me to quit without being shamed by him. He let my best in that moment be enough. I gave my best and his best, and he let me move on. These were things I had always denied I needed because I knew I wouldn't get them.

Up until Ron said it, and even after, I never thought of that training session as a start. I didn't think of myself as a beginner. I discounted the fact I would get better if I kept doing it. If I showed up and did the work.

I was so used to trying for a little while and not seeing the number on the scale go down, I didn't believe in "better." Because I didn't see the "better" I wanted to see—a lower number on the scale—I forgot about the other "betters" that show up even when the scale stays the same: doing more reps, completing a circuit faster, having more energy at the end of a workout, being able to get deeper into a stretch, my clothes fitting better, etc.

My fitness assessment with Ron can be compared with my experiences with "moving on" after a breakup. I was single the first twenty-two years of my life. I knew how to be single. I expected being single again to be like riding a bike. It would be natural. The knowledge of how to do it would be such a part of me, I wouldn't even have to think about it. However, the reality, like my session with Ron, revealed I was more out of practice than I thought.

The job of a personal trainer is to help you reach your fitness goals, not anyone else's. It's their job to determine when to increase the weight or the reps, and when to change up your diet or workout routine to keep you from hitting a plateau. It's their job to challenge you, but as I learned with Ron, it's also their job to know when you've given it your all and need to rest or move on to something else.

You need personal training to get fit in other areas besides fitness. Just like you may need to see a personal trainer to help you lose weight, or a financial planner to get your finances in order, you may need to see a licensed mental health counselor (LMHC) or therapist after a traumatic event or major life transition. You may need to seek professional assistance to become fit enough to make decisions regarding relationships, or to trust your decision making. Just as there's no shame seeing a physician when you're sick or a personal trainer when you need help losing weight, there should be no shame in seeking professional help for general guidance and direction, depression, anxiety, or suicidal ideations.

God is the Great Physician, but there are people God has set in place to assist us with our emotional and spiritual health and fitness. God blessed these individuals with an ability to help people heal mentally, spiritually and/or emotionally. You should not enter a relationship with anyone else until you're fit mentally, spiritually, and emotionally.

Every client a personal trainer sees doesn't require the same routine. Some can follow a written plan, while others need one on one sessions with the trainer to stay on track. In the same way, people who need the services of a mental, spiritual, or emotional trainer will require different types of assistance. Be open to whatever level of assistance you need and accept it. This may mean seeking wise counsel from brothers and sisters in Christ or seeing an LMHC.

Make sure you also take care of yourself physically. Don't drown your problems in food, starve yourself, self-medicate with alcohol, prescription drugs or illegal substances, binge watch trashy TV, go out clubbing, or chase other destructive pursuits. Utilize positive ways to sublimate feelings and reassign mental energy, like exercise, pursuing a hobby or volunteering.

FITNESS DEMANDS DISCIPLINE

Some people are motivated to keep doing things because of the results. The bible tells us this about Christ. It says that for the joy set before Him, He endured the cross, despising the shame (Heb. 12:2). Christ was tempted in all points like we are, yet without sin (Heb. 4:15). He had the same distractions available—entertainment, relationships, people—yet he stayed the course for what was set before him.

What I've tended to do is pursue something I might enjoy doing and attempt to use it to get where I want to go. This is not the biblical example. This doesn't mean you can't enjoy the journey. It means the destination, not the enjoyment of the journey, is what you're chasing.

The result of living a life led by the Lord is desirable, but much of the process is painful. The life of a Christian running to obtain the prize requires discipline.

> [4] In your struggle against sin you have not yet resisted to the point of shedding your blood. [5] And have you forgotten the exhortation that addresses you as sons?
>
> "My son, do not regard lightly the discipline of the Lord, nor be weary when reproved by him. [6] For the

Lord disciplines the one he loves, and chastises every son whom he receives."

[7] It is for discipline that you have to endure. God is treating you as sons. For what son is there whom his father does not discipline? [8] If you are left without discipline, in which all have participated, then you are illegitimate children and not sons. [9] Besides this, we have had earthly fathers who disciplined us and we respected them. Shall we not much more be subject to the Father of spirits and live? [10] For they disciplined us for a short time as it seemed best to them, but he disciplines us for our good, that we may share his holiness. [11] For the moment all discipline seems painful rather than pleasant, but later it yields the peaceful fruit of righteousness to those who have been trained by it. Heb. 12:4-11

The Hebrew writer focuses in on the person, purpose, and product of discipline in this passage. Each area adds another layer to our understanding of the role of discipline in developing our fitness.

♥ PERSON

There are two people involved in discipline: God and the Christian. God, like any father, disciplines His children. God disciplines those He loves and receives as sons and daughters. God's discipline validates our legitimacy as His children.

The Christian is exhorted to endure discipline. They shouldn't become weary of God's reproof or correction. Paul writes about having the discipline of an athlete to exercise self-control and discipline his body. A Christian must discipline himself as well as endure God's discipline.

♥ PURPOSE

The purpose of discipline can't be separated from the person of God or the product it produces. The purposes of discipline are to validate our status as heirs of God, develop us, and train us. God disciplines us so that we might share His holiness. Discipline's purpose isn't to be pleasant, but to produce something in us.

♥ PRODUCT

Discipline is painful. The process of being disciplined hurts, but the product of discipline is pleasant. The peaceful fruit of righteousness, share God's holiness, and winning the crown when we have finished our race is worth the unpleasantness of enduring discipline.

When you experience with chastisement and God's discipline, remember who is disciplining you, the reason He is reproving and chastising you, and the fruit the discipline will yield. There is no fitness without discipline.

NEW HAIR. WHO DIS? AKA PACE YOURSELF

As women, our hair, clothes, and makeup (or lack thereof) are a part of our identity. The way we dress or wear our hair might be cited as the reason we haven't found a spouse as often as any internal failing. The pressure to maintain a certain weight or look a certain way to attract a mate can crush the spirit of a woman who feels like she doesn't measure up.

A woman's looks are constantly scrutinized. They can be a major source of insecurity, pride, comparison, or competition for women. How a woman looks can impact more than her dating prospects. It can factor into employment opportunities, social status, and treatment by the opposite sex in social situations.

People can assume changing your hairstyle is an effort to try something new or a cry for help. People might believe a woman who cuts off all her hair has gone crazy a la Britney Spears, a woman who gets a dramatic haircut is "going through something," or a brunette who stops dying her hair blonde is "letting herself go." It's possible for a woman to cut her hair because she prefers it short. A natural brunette may stop dying her hair to embrace a more natural look. A change in hairstyle doesn't have to make sense to anyone but the woman who wants to wear it.

Coco Chanel saw a woman changing her hair as the first step in changing her life. I wore my hair in the same three styles all my adult life: in a ponytail, flat ironed straight, or in braids. When I moved out of Orlando, I found a new hairstylist. I could tell she loved what she did, and she was good at it. When she asked what style I wanted, I paused. Here was an expert hairstylist who loved making women look their best. She knows more about what looks good than I do. I knew what I was comfortable with, what was functional, but I realized in that moment how much I had limited myself over the years. "I want a style that looks like me."

As I sat in the stylist's chair, she didn't just do my hair; she healed a little bit of my heart. She spoke about the beauty of my hair and handled it like a bolt of fine fabric. She marveled at my natural curl pattern. She praised my features and called attention to areas of attractiveness I overlooked in the mirror each morning. Having someone point out all the positives instead of picking at my flaws was uplifting and empowering.

When I saw my hair for the first time, I was blown away. The hairstyle did more than tame my mane; it framed my face perfectly. I could see a sparkle of confidence in my eyes. For the first time in years, I was confident in how I looked. I looked like me, and I liked it. That's what a new hairstyle did for me.

Every change you make after a breakup doesn't have to be soul deep. Every step of self-discovery doesn't have to be a life-altering event. Part of the process of uncovering and reasserting identity is trying new things. Changing your hairstyle or trying on an outfit in a color you normally wouldn't wear are simple ways to start stepping out of your comfort zone. Pace yourself. Don't ignore the deep dives, but feel free to float on the surface every now and then.

Here are a few other things you might want to change up in this season:

♥ **Foods/diet.** Try a new restaurant, recipe, or regimen. Surprise your taste buds. Wake them up with new flavors. Make your stomach smile with foods that taste good and are good for your body. Get creative.

♥ **Exercise programs.** Try a class or exercise you've never tried before. Revisit a style you haven't tried in a while. Don't talk yourself out of trying something new or engage in negative self-talk about what you can't do. Don't worry about what anyone else in the gym or on the trail is thinking. Most people who love exercising cheer on people who are trying. People who hate exercising are focused on trying not to die as they finish their workout. The rest are thinking about what they've done or what they still need to do, inwardly rocking out to the music playing in their headphones, or focused on something else that doesn't involve you.

♥ **Solo travel.** I went on several solo trips after my relationship ended. This was something I'd never done before. I went to places I'd never visited and stayed overnight alone. It was so much fun to plan my days and go where I wanted. Go to that place you were hoping you and your ex would go. Visit a new city, a new place in your city, or a new part of your state. You can find new places to explore from news segments like Florida on a Tankful. They will frequently feature a place or activity you've never heard of that is located a short drive away.

♥ **Concerts, Conferences and Congregations.** One of the first events I attended after my relationship ended was the National Academy of Christian A cappella Music Awards (NACAMA). Spending the weekend being filled up with good music, meeting new people, and being in a spiritual environment was soothing to my soul. I felt hopeful and invigorated. I've attended many conferences, visited many congregations, and enjoyed many concerts since then. I never fail to meet people with similar interests and passions. I encourage you to get out there. Find something you're interested in and go where others who love that thing gather together. It doesn't have to be a church event. Attend an art gallery opening. Go to a conference for women in technology. Go to Comic Con. Don't be afraid to grab a girlfriend and go, or to attend alone.

STRENGTH TRAINING

While a breakup may disrupt your life, your life doesn't stop moving to allow you time to process what's happened. There's little to no time to complain about it or dwell on how unfair things are. If you did have the time, the weight of your feelings could crush you if you haven't built up the muscle strength to shoulder such a heavy burden.

Sometimes our feelings have feelings about what we're going through, but other people are depending on us to do a job, mother them, or be there for them, so we push those feelings aside. This method may work for a while, but understand, avoiding feelings will keep you from true wholeness. At some point, you will have to confront and conquer your emotions to achieve true emotional health and fitness.

I delved deeply into spiritual fitness after my breakup. I prayed regularly. I read the bible. I visited the sick. I attended conference. I poured into my sisters in Christ. But even while this strengthened me spiritually, junk was working its way into other areas of my life that eventually stagnated my spiritual fitness. Most of this junk was entering through weak spots in my emotional sphere.

My lack of emotional strength affected my spiritual, physical and financial health as I sought to build up muscle in other parts of me to compensate for my weak emotional state.

Reading the bible helped me tremendously. Visiting the sick and shut in shifted my perspective and gave me a positive outlet. But using those things to avoid feeling and dealing with my breakup, strained and overworked my spiritual muscles.

I can tell you from experience, you will never be fit enough to outrun your problems forever. There will be a season when you have too much free time and those deficiencies will have an opportunity to creep up on you. They will sit and stay for a while. You're going to be confronted with seasons of the same storms again and again until you deal with the trauma and heal.

As fit as you may be, you will reach the end of your strength. The wonderful thing about God is He can step in where your strength ends. His strength is made perfect in your weakness; in other words, when you are weak, that's when you can experience Him at His strongest. He will heal you when you submit to Him. When it's clear you have nothing left and it's not your strength propelling, keeping, or sustaining you, but God's—that's when He will get the glory.

TIPS FOR BEING FIT

1. **Make time.** My aunt goes to the gym three days a week, even though she owns a business and her workday starts before her gym time. No matter what we're doing, she schedules things around being able to go to the gym for an hour Monday, Wednesday, and Friday. It helps her mentally. Make time for your emotional and spiritual fitness the same way. Schedule time to read your bible, journal, read devotionals, go on walks with the Lord, pray—anything that contributes to you emotionally or spiritually. Sit with a counselor for an hour. Put it on your schedule and commit to keeping your appointment.

2. **Learn Discipline.** Read **Celebration of Discipline** by Richard J. Foster to learn about Christian spiritual disciplines. Find a good book on spiritual gifts—what they are, if they are still in effect, and how to cultivate them. You can't exercise something you don't know is there. Learn what spiritual muscles to target and what exercises to do to build them up. Sit with a minister or elder from your church to learn more about spiritual gifts and disciplines. Sit with some of your friends and ask them what you're good at.

3. **Drink plenty of water.** Read the word of God. Christ tells the woman at the well if she had known who He was and asked, He would give her living water that would spring up in her and she would never thirst again (John 4:10, 13-14). Hydration is important to health and fitness. You need water to live. You can go longer without eating than you can without water. Similarly, you can't survive without the living water, the word of God. You must take in God's word constantly. You can do this through a bible app that reads the bible to you while you're exercising, driving or going about your day. You can listen to podcasts of bible studies

and sermons. You can listen while you're doing other things. But for me, I need to read it. I need to see it. I need to connect the sight and sound in my brain. For those who write need to right, Cultivate What Matters has a collection of Write the Word journals which may help you connect with the word.

4. **Learn your strengths and weaknesses, and work on strengthening them.** Many people learn to see their weaknesses as boundaries, marking off areas they shouldn't explore. They stay in the comfort zone of their strengths where they feel safe and in control. But the only way to improve is to strengthen areas in which you are weak. Athletes shift from good to great when they focus on strengthening weaknesses their opponents have exploited in the past. Just like an athlete seeks to exploit an opponent's weakness, the devil seeks out your weakest points to attack. Prepare for him by building up and fortifying those areas.

FIT TEST

It's easy to misjudge your mental, spiritual, and emotional fitness levels. You might think you're ready to get back into the dating pool, but before you jump in the deep end, make sure you remember how to swim. You don't want to realize you're not ready to date in the middle of an awkward meal with a virtual stranger. There's a better way to judge your readiness for a relationship: give yourself a fitness test.

The workout program Insanity begins and ends with a fitness test. You record how well you do on Day One and compare your results to what you can do at Day Ninety. A fit test makes it easy to see how much progress you've made.

If you're wondering if it's time for you to start dating again, ask yourself the following "Dating Fitness Test" questions:

- ❤ Have you received closure?
- ❤ Do you know and acknowledge your role in the relationship and its collapse?
- ❤ Have the things broken by your breakup been restored, replaced or rejoiced over?
- ❤ What state are your non-romantic relationships in?
- ❤ Do you avoid language that condemns your ex or vindicates yourself when referring to your past relationship?
- ❤ Have you forgiven your ex?
- ❤ Have you forgiven yourself?
- ❤ Do you think of your ex as a brother in Christ (if Christian)?
- ❤ Have you stopped stalking their social media and/or making subliminal posts?
- ❤ How have you addressed the issues your breakup uncovered?
- ❤ Why do you want to pursue a new relationship? Is this a good reason to resume dating?

There are a million other questions you may need to ask and answer before you feel ready to pursue another relationship. My heart for you is that you will embrace everything you've learned about yourself and your Savior through this process and proceed into the future, looking to and trusting in Him, no matter what happens in your romantic life.

XOXO,
Erica D. Hearns (Your Break Buddy)

Acknowledgements

Writing a book, like walking through a breakup, can feel like a solitary experience. It's only after you've reached a point of healing and look back down the road that you realize how many people have been beside you—some silently sharing the load, others walking with you a short while, and still others cheering you on from the sidelines waving signs decorated with words of encouragement. I'm standing at the end of this book journey tired and breathless, but also in awe of the company I've had every step of the way.

God, I thank You for being close to the brokenhearted, and for sending your Son to heal our broken hearts, no matter the cause of our brokenness. I thank You for giving me a powerful message of wholeness and restoration and returning to You and Your original intent for our lives to share with other women who need to hear it. I thank you for putting each person, place and thing in my life that I will thank here and those I thank you for in my thoughts and prayers who have impacted my life.

I would like to thank my "breakthrough crew," the women and men who made my breakup season more fun and rewarding than I ever thought possible: Mom, my biggest cheerleader and strongest supporter, who hears all of my ideas well before they are fully formed and knows every change I made to this book from start to finish (sorry); Tasha Blomenkamp, my roommate and friend in the fiercest part of the storm; Jenny Bullard, the supportive and fair-minded friend I hope I can grow to become; my book club ladies: Marilyn, Miriam, Victoria, Yolanda, Andreana, and Ariel A.; my Aunt Louise, who has always been there when I've needed her, and who is always ready to give an opinion on a concept, cover, or title; my Reserved Singles Conference room 606 ladies: Jessica, Ryanne, and Ariel S.; the Concord St. Church of Christ ladies bible class and women's retreat group; the Sunday after church visiting crew: Sister Antranique Johnson, Brother Joshua Drummer, Brother Harvey Drummer III, Brother Roderick Harris, Brother Omega Austin, Brother Harvey Drummer, Jr. and many others previously mentioned; Sister Juanita Saintelian, Sister Gaylin Thomas, Sister Tanya Drummer, Sister Pearl McFarland, Sis. Brenda Calloway, Sister Paulette Morgan, my Westmoreland Dr. Church of Christ family, and my Avon Park Church of Christ family; and the ladies in the Wholehearted Ladies Facebook group. Special thanks to Anthony Blunt and Syndy Colebrook for having me on their radio shows and introducing me to their audiences.

I must also thank several people for their specific contributions to this book: the lovely ladies who so generously shared about their breakup experiences: Katie, Kacy, Natalie, Ayanna, Erica U., Kelsey, Cheryl, Andreana, and Nichole. I know your willingness to share will bear fruit in the lives of the women who read your words; my father, Edward Hearns, my faithful first reader; Alexandra Rousseau, my dear friend from high school to present day. You have no idea how our conversations pushed this book to be more than I thought it could be. Your commitment to seek the Lord and your sweet spirit have impacted this book, but more importantly, my life. April D. Wesley, who provided me with advice and encouragement on how to approach writing about the pain of my past with purpose; the Reserved Singles' Conference, which presented me with many opportunities to go deeper and really dig in to the concept of doing relationships God's way; the dynamic Juliette Bush, who supported the vision of this book and helped me bring it to fruition by introducing me to my cover designer. Your heart for encouragement is unmatched; Norbert Elnar, my cover designer. You took a vague concept and an even vaguer vision and created something special. Thank you for using your immense talent to bring my vision to life; everyone who critiqued cover options along the way: Erica's Book Launch Bunch, my critique buddies, Dana and Christina, the Christian Indie Authors Facebook group, April, and Keith (lil' bro.). Your input was much appreciated.

While many of the above made me tear up thinking about how they supported my vision, there are other things that contributed to this book that I would like to thank publicly here: Twix (the dog, not the candy), a faithful friend and companion who went on long walks with me and stuck by my side while I worked out what my breakup meant; Panera Bread, for keeping me fueled with decaf caramel lattes with extra caramel, and for being the place where I first typed words about my breakup and the place I penned the bulk of my author's note/introduction; the Diplomat Beach Resort Hollywood, where I wrote my heart out one morning and felt pampered for the first time in a long time; room 606 in the Hilton Bonnet Creek, where I spent several mornings transcribing and editing parts of this book; my iPhone, iPod, and RCA digital recorder, where I recorded ramblings and captured the major concepts of this book; that random twitter post that asked "what is more painful than a breakup?"; and Domino's, cherry 7Up, and Tahitian Treat, the true MVPs of my writing life (along with the occasional Olive Garden Steak Gorgonzola Alfredo).

Altered before the Altar: Allowing God to Make You "Meet" to be Met is an invitation to an altered life. Learn God's design for your single season, biblically based principles of mate selection, and red flags to look for by studying scripture and wisdom from real life Christian couples, psychologists, ministers, and elders. Are you prepared to be presented to the man God has for you? If not, then it's time to get **Altered**!

Praise for Altered before the Altar

"Inspired me to take my faith to the next level."

"Like sitting down with your best friend or favorite aunt."

"Straightforward talk seasoned with kindness and concern"

"Necessary."

"Beautifully written with convicting and encouraging insight"

Available on my website, www.aseriousseason.com/shop

$11.99 print
$7.99 eBook (Enter promo code **GETALTERED** at checkout).

Also available on Amazon and Barnes &Noble
$14.99 Print
$9.99 eBook

The **Altered before the Altar‧ Devotional Study Guide** is the perfect complement to Altered before the Altar. Pointed discussion questions, detailed exercises, and thought-provoking devotionals and prompts aid you in applying key concepts and principles to your life and relationships. You've read about being altered; now it's time to get altered!

Available on my website, www.aseriousseason.com/shop

$7.49 print

Also available on Amazon and Barnes &Noble

$7.50 Print

The Perfect Pair!

Grab the Altered set for $20.00

Includes
Bookmark
Print
and Single Season Survival Pack

Erica D. Hearns

The Season for Getting Serious:
Growing Intimacy with Christ in Any Season

"You were running well; who hindered you?"

Many Christian women want a deeper relationship with God, but they can't seem to grow intimacy with Him. They start out with intention, but they are distracted and knocked off course by their life's circumstances and responsibilities.

The Season for Getting Serious: Growing Intimacy with Christ in any Season, encourages and equips women to grow closer to Christ in whatever season they find themselves in. This is not another checklist or New Year's resolution; it's a clarion call to the woman of God to stop waiting--for a new year, better circumstances, or less distractions--and start growing in this season of their lives--right now.

The Season for Getting Serious speaks to the woman in the middle, on the run, grieving, or suffering from spiritual disease. It speaks to women wrestling with doubt, success, and burying the old man. This book whispers to the heart of every woman seeking Christ in the middle of the muck and mess of life and calls her out of the darkness into His marvelous light. Available on my website, www.aseriousseason.com/shop

$14.99 print

$6.49 eBook

Enter promo code **MYSEASON** at checkout.

Also available on Amazon and Barnes &Noble

$19.99 Print

$9.99 eBook

Jump Start the Journey: Put Pen to Paper, Perfect the Publication Process, and Promote for Propulsion

Do you have a book in you?

Have you felt called to write, but are unsure where to begin? Have you written a manuscript but don't know how to get it in readers' hands? Don't allow another day, month, or year to pass by without writing or publishing your book! Jumpstart the Journey offers aspiring authors encouragement and education on penning, publishing, and promoting their non-fiction works.

In this workbook you will learn how to:

- Write the book of your heart in record time.
- Elevate your content from good to great.
- Avoid costly setbacks and rack up successes
- Find and augment your audience

And much more.

This workbook will call you out, call you up and convict you in the best ways to use your voice and your victories to bring glory and honor to God.

$19.99 print (Enter promo code **JUMPSTART** at checkout).

ABOUT SERIOUS SEASON PRESS

Since its beginning as the blog The Season for Getting Serious in 2014, the aim of Serious Season Press has been to provide tools to support women seriously seeking the Savior in every season of life. Serious Season Press produces books, bible studies, journals, prints and accessories whose sole purpose is to promote and propel a personal relationship with Christ.

ABOUT SERIOUS SEASON PUBLISHING SERVICES

Serious Season Publishing Services sprang from Erica's desire to better serve Christians seeking to share their stories. Serious Season Publishing services provides book coaching, editing, formatting, and publishing services to assist writers with bringing their books to life. Authors can find pricing information and free resources on www.aseriousseason.com/SeriousPub.